INSIDE OUTSIDE

INSIDE OUTSIDE

A SOURCEBOOK *of* INSPIRED GARDEN ROOMS

LINDA O'KEEFFE

Timber Press
Portland, Oregon

FRONTISPIECE On the exterior kitchen wall of Carl D'Aquino and Bernd Goeckler's Hudson Valley house, ceramic wall plaques created by Alexandre Bigot in the 1930s echo the style of the interior's furnishings and help obliterate the distinction between the garden and the front porch.

OPPOSITE In Robert Couturier's Connecticut garden, a bronze table and chairs create an impromptu room at the base of stairs surrounded by shapely bushes.

Copyright © 2019 by Linda O'Keeffe. All rights reserved.
Photography credits appear on page 245.

Published in 2019 by Timber Press, Inc.

The Haseltine Building
133 S.W. Second Avenue, Suite 450
Portland, Oregon 97204-3527
timberpress.com

Printed in China

Jacket design by Claudia Brandenburg/Language Arts

ISBN 978-1-60469-826-8

Catalog records for this book are available from the
Library of Congress and the British Library.

CONTENTS

INTRODUCTION

OPPOSITE Two fences covered with star jasmine or Japanese silverberry converge in Scott Flax's Santa Monica garden. They provide a backdrop for a set of teak chairs in a sitting area where Flax covered a side table with antique Portuguese tiles and placed a bowl created by Philip Maberry and Scott Walker.

Thanks to a glass wall, a cube chair in the living room of a California house designed by Charles Allum appears to be a three-dimensional continuation of a white terrazzo and grass checkerboard floor in an adjacent courtyard.

IN A QUEST TO SATISFY THEIR CLIENTS' NESTING INSTINCTS, interior and landscape designers share an aesthetic lexicon. As space planners, they both rely on structure and think of soft and hard materials, color, texture, lighting, and accessories as everyday tools. They consider circulation, visual pacing, procession, and flow. They configure and decorate walls and install furniture. They edit, edit, edit or weed, weed, weed. The basic thought processes behind the design of a hall, a corridor, a pathway, and an allée are interchangeable—doors and gates serve the same purpose, and there's little difference between laying a stone floor in a kitchen or in a courtyard.

It is quaint to think of a garden as a house's appendage rather than its continuation, and this book treats the two as sides of the same coin. In some cases, a house flows seamlessly into its surroundings, but even when indoor and outdoor spaces aren't literal extensions of each other, they can share a sensibility. Interior designers often look to nature when they choose color schemes, and for some, including Barbara Barry, whose interiors often wear the "colors of the earth dressed up to live inside," that symbiosis has developed into a signature style. Since time immemorial, interior and landscape designers have inspired one another. When celebrated author and garden designer Luciano Giubbilei first ventured into horticulture in the mid-1990s, his gardens were heavily influenced by interior décor. He was particularly enamored with the work of Christian Liaigre, of whom he recalled, "There was a movement, a dynamic in the way he arranged a room . . . with one piece that would break the symmetry and the stiffness within his compositions."

All gardens represent a valiant attempt to tame our immediate environment, both to embrace nature and keep her at bay. A logical way to organize any space—be it a meadow or a gymnasium-size loft—is to break it down into manageable portions, or rooms. This technique is as old as the hills. It's identifiable in Persian quadrant layouts, in ancient Egyptian courtyards, and in Baroque parterres. In this book, I define a "room" in loose terms. The word

suggests conventional structure—walls, floor, and ceiling—and, needless to say, I've included lanais, pergolas, porches, pavilions, arbors, terraces, and loggias. But I've expanded the concept of an exterior room to encompass gardens I discovered where there's a suggestion of shelter, a palpable sense of enclosure, or a feeling of containment whether its structure is actual or implied.

To me, an outdoor room is any place where our impulse to eat, lounge, watch birds, contemplate, cook, exercise, swim, play games, read, paint, sightsee, sculpt, leaf peep, stargaze, meditate, or do absolutely nothing is accommodated. In my mind, the love of living outside requires no more than an open attitude and a reverence for nature. It's delightful to take an afternoon nap on a sleeping porch attached to a house or in a hammock strung between two trees, but it's exquisite to lay down in a clearing in the woods under dappled shade with an ear lightly pressed against a pillow of fragrant moss.

William Morris, the nineteenth-century poet and textile designer who believed in marrying a dwelling to its setting, coined the phrase "carpet garden-ing" to describe formulaic, non-site–specific landscapes, and you won't find any of those in this book. What you will find are unique reflections of each gardener's personality. Some gardens will invite you to sit and relax, while others will beg to be admired from afar; each one is meant to be experienced and enjoyed with all the senses. When Harold Nicolson conceived of Sissinghurst, one of England's most treasured gardens, he referred to the ten distinctive rooms he and Vita Sackville-West created there as a "succession of privacies." I insert "intimate" and "passionate" into that phrase as I describe the projects in this book.

Neither a garden nor an interior is ever finished. One evolves because it is alive, and the other evolves as long as it is lived in. Each reflects and is affected by time in its own way. Textiles fade, lose their crispness, and become thread-bare; flowers wilt and die. With the aid of skillful editing and time-lapse

CLOCKWISE, FROM TOP LEFT:

In the Hudson Valley garden owned by Patrick Sears and Jeffrey Williams, a cloak of Dutchman's pipe (*Aristolochia macrophylla*) and kiwi (*Actinidia arguta*) softens the corner of a century-old barn the way floor-to-ceiling curtains add flowing lines to an interior wall.

In temperate climates, nature's air-conditioning (the shade of a tree) often determines the location of an outdoor dining room.

Highly pruned hedges, a single chair, and an armillary sphere create an al fresco room in this Hudson, New York, garden.

When Marjorie Skouras, a former movie set designer, turned her eye to interiors, she used artificial boxwood topiaries to transform this master bedroom's generic bed into a four poster.

photography, television makeovers renovate and furnish whole houses within a few days, when, in fact, an authentic living room, like a real garden, evolves and matures gradually. Because of time's relationship to growth, buying a plant and buying a piece of furniture are two very different propositions. Unlike a tree canopy, a bed canopy will never spread its wings; a dining table doesn't seasonally shed its leaves; and a floral carpet would be ruined if it were given the amount of water a carpet of real snowdrops and crocuses requires.

No scented candle or diffuser could ever duplicate petrichor, an obscure term concocted to signify the distinctive fragrance arising from dry earth after a downpour of rain. The word's derivation alludes to the fluid flowing through the veins of mythological gods arguably because the heavenly, intoxicating smell of earth defies an everyday description. An entreaty in Frances Hodgson Burnett's *The Secret Garden*, "Might I have a bit of earth?" echoes a primal urge to experience nature firsthand and be healed by its wonders. Every gardener featured in this book knows exactly how that feels. ↓

SPACE

OPPOSITE The openness of
landscaper Mark Streiter and
architect Tony Machado's
Hudson, New York, garden
prompted them to invite
ninety friends for dinner and
dance one summer evening.

A pair of side-by-side chairs
in Patrick Sears and Jeffrey
Williams's upstate New York
garden lends human scale
and intimacy.

DESIGNERS APPROACH NEW PROJECTS IN SIMILAR WAYS. As they walk
through a house, apartment, or garden and study it from every angle, they
evaluate its structure and contemplate how to reinforce its strengths and
downplay its weaknesses. As they consider the site, they assign a function to
each distinct area and envision paints, furniture, and textiles—or flowers and
shrubs—expressing its mood, attitude, and style. When the design of any small
space is resolved, it can serve as a valuable template, because, inside and out,
the most efficient floor plans invariably break down the overall into a series
of small spaces or rooms. Paradoxically, once it's apportioned, a garden or
an interior appears to be larger than it actually is because whenever it's not
possible to size up its total dimensions or square footage in one fell swoop,
mystery sets in because there's no telling what lies beyond.

A great room or loft is the indoor equivalent of a large garden, where no
structure exists beyond its perimeter walls. In an open-plan house, a carpet may
establish where a living room begins and ends, just as a lawn may define a play-
ground's boundaries. A work island can separate a dining room from a kitchen,
just as a row of topiaries or a change in levels performs the same service outside.
The fresh air counterpart to an open bookcase defining a private corner of a
room is an arbor or trellis demarcating one section of a garden from the rest.

Whenever we cross a threshold, we instinctively scope out the proportions of
what we're about to walk into. If it's a confined area, we adjust our sight range
and move our bodies more efficiently. When we encounter an expanse, we search

for a scale we can relate to in human terms. One exception is if we are on top of a mountain, beside the ocean, or in an open, rolling meadow. Then our comparative smallness can provoke awe, especially when we're able to appreciate nature's majesty. Because our vision becomes more panoramic when we're outside, the scale of traditional garden furniture tends to be on the large side. Wide stairs and ample doorways might feel cartoonish inside, but outside they're appropriate. Eating a meal under a pergola that's four times the size of our lunch counter feels comfortable rather than alienating or abnormally grand, because we're beneath a ceiling of sky. Interestingly enough, psychologically there's little difference between actual and perceived spaciousness. They're equally pleasing.

It's disconcerting to enter a building and not understand its floor plan, but not knowing a garden's layout holds intrigue and adventure; when we imagine it to be large, even when it's not, the mind relaxes into exploration mode and the body follows suit. Knowing how to alter the way a space is perceived is basic to every designer's skill set. They know how to visually stretch a path or a hallway as it leads away so it appears to be longer; they can play with our notions of depth and dimension by using dark or light colors or by positioning a large object in the foreground or a small object way off in the distance close to an imagined horizon. They can neutralize a feeling of claustrophobia and imply more square footage by hanging a mirror or a piece of artwork with a wide or deep perspective.

Inside and out, stripes and line repetitions—the man-made and natural kinds—are versatile shape shifters. Depending on whether they're vertical, as in a picket fence or in the clustered stalks of a bamboo grove, or horizontal, such as a wide set of steps or anything paralleling the horizon, they can visually elongate, widen, narrow, heighten, stretch, or shorten the size of any wall, curtain, carpet, lawn, fence, trellis, pergola, doorway, or path.

Japanese landscape designers have the *miegakure* technique at their disposal and often use it to conceal and reveal parts of a landscape just as screens and curtains cover and open up aspects of an interior. Whenever something is hidden, it's human nature for curiosity to prompt us to wonder or wander. ✧

OPPOSITE In a garden close to the beach in Corona del Mar, California, designer James Magni positioned a ceramic fire pit where it would cast its light onto an outdoor living area, much like an interior hall pendant would illuminate an adjacent room.

BELOW, FROM LEFT TO RIGHT:

The treads, risers, and railings of interior steps have to comply with building codes, but outside it's invariably a question of choosing the proportions that work well visually.

A freestanding, antique set of gates and a fence on Carl D'Aquino's New York property don't enclose anything. They're simply used as a narrative device to control the garden's energetic flow.

A solid, closed gate implies more space, but a closed gate with open metalwork teases at what lies ahead.

LINE DRAWING

ONE OF THE FIRST THINGS MATT LARKIN DID after he bought a classic 1839 Greek Revival house on four acres in Richmond, Massachusetts, was to visually extend its vestibule into the garden. Standing just outside the front door's threshold, he placed a transit level on a tripod and pointed it away from the house's central axis. Treating its beam as a guideline, he set a pole 500 feet away and designated planting spots for two rows of sapling crabapple trees. Taking his cue from André Le Nôtre at Versailles, he built in a false perspective; the first two trees are 20 feet apart and the last pair are 15 feet apart. Now, nearly three decades later, the majestic allée reaches high into the heavens and, from certain angles, appears to stretch into infinity.

Larkin, board chairman of the Berkshire Botanical Garden in Stockbridge, Massachusetts, appreciates other peoples' wild, rambling gardens, but his own is guided by principles of balance and symmetry, much like the orderly, square configuration of the rooms in his house. As a principal of Grant Larkin, an interior design firm he owns with his wife, Lainie Grant, he filled the couple's house with an edited, quirky mix of antiques and contemporary art. All the interiors he designs feel authentic in large part due to a group of artisans—blacksmiths, seamstresses, bronze-casters—who detail his furnishings. He treats his garden accessories with the same respect so, for example, his iron girding mahogany planters are as sturdy as chests.

The celebrated designer David Hicks inspired elements inside and out; Larkin considers Hicks's book, *My Kind of Garden* (1999), a bible, much like Russell Page's *The Education of a Gardener* (1962). Over the years, Larkin has added several structures to the property and it currently contains a transplanted nineteenth-century barn, a teahouse constructed from locust posts, a saltwater pool, and a spacious pavilion, which serves as a shady, alfresco living room. Larkin tempers the garden's decorum with some eccentricity, and there's a huge field where he fashions fantastical topiary forms around welded steel cages. There's also his eye-popping use of color. Shocks of red (as green's complementary color) appear on everything from axial gates surrounding the pool to a powder-coated, coral-inspired chinoiserie sofa in the pavilion.

He also loves black and describes his proclivity for pairing it with red as "Dorothy Draper meets the Hell's Angels." In fact, he thinks of a coat of black paint as a failsafe solution if ever one of his designs feels unresolved. Inside, when he paints window sashes black, the frames recede and the view

OPPOSITE On occasion, when Matt Larkin dyes the pool water in his Massachusetts garden black, its deep, mirrored surface reflects the garden's strict symmetry.

Sets of red metal gates surrounding the pool and its pavilion repeat the color of a nearby barn's standing seam metal roof.

PREVIOUS SPREAD An experimental "topiary yard," where Larkin builds fantastical shapes on metal forms he crafts by hand, resembles a surreal chess room. It's where rows of boxwood pyramids are crowned with leafy, bushy-tailed squirrels and a pruned yew obelisk wears a bird-shaped hat.

BELOW Dutchman's pipe vines (*Aristolochia macrophylla*) will eventually cover the roof and columns of the pool pavilion, where pots of silver grass, bromeliads, and tree ferns mingle with the odd plaster gnome.

OPPOSITE A vase of sunflowers sits on a glass table beneath Larkin's crystal-and-wire chandelier assemblage. Red-lacquered couches define the outdoor room's perimeter and nod to the red gates surrounding the pool.

becomes more immediate. Outside, black gateposts render definitive vertical lines that also seem to get absorbed into the landscape. He even pours black Pylam dye into the swimming pool to temporarily transform its surface into a shiny onyx mirror. Needless to say, he loves black flowers, particularly 'Queen of the Night' tulips, black hellebores, chocolate cosmos, 'Black Velvet' petunias, and black hollyhocks, which transform themselves into shadows when arranged together in a vase. ⇃

FROM LEFT TO RIGHT:

Punctuated by a patinated putto, a studded wooden doorway at the end of a rippled Indiana limestone pathway leads to the pool and enforces the concept of the garden as a series of interconnecting rooms.

Another of Larkin's follies, a ten-foot-tall Japanese yew colonnade with five-foot-high finials, is positioned to align with the pavilion.

A second gate leads to a field of *Hydrangea paniculata* 'Tardiva', where spherical box-woods and cypress hedges are decoratively studded with round security mirrors.

LEFT Shortly after he acquired the property, Larkin grew an allée of crabapple trees from whips. Every other year, they are pollarded.

ABOVE A cast-iron stag produced by J. W. Fiske in the nineteenth century watches over the pool in line with the garden's prominent axis.

Symmetry

Symmetry, an even distribution of visual weight measured from a central line or axis, exudes dignity and stability. Whether it's a pair of candlesticks arranged on either end of a mantelpiece, matching combinations of bedside tables and lamps, or an allée of trees, as in Matt Larkin's garden, we perceive it as resolved and complete. Whenever symmetry is overdone, when it's too perfect and precise, it can feel staid and impersonal. Radial symmetry is found in a central light fixture, a table surrounded by evenly spaced chairs, or a sunflower. Larkin applied it to raised vegetable beds shaped into quadrants and in the four axial gates around his pool pavilion, and in both cases its effect is calming. ⬇

GREENHOUSE AFFECT

ALEX MECONI'S VENICE, CALIFORNIA, GARDEN isn't strictly outside, and its attached house isn't exactly an interior space. Thanks to a sliding glass wall, they are both inside and outside at one and the same time. After Meconi, an architect, leveled a dilapidated cottage on the property, he thought about replacing it with his version of a Balinese pavilion. His final maquette, or model, however, was more severe and modernist, and the built house resembles two shoeboxes stacked at right angles. The lower level expands into a courtyard bordered with exotic plants and shrubs, and the plot appears to be situated in the midst of a jungle when in fact it's a short bike ride from the beach.

Meconi acquired his fondness for tropical greenery in South America, where he was born and where the Brazilian landscape designer Roberto Burle Marx, whose extravagant gardens resembled wild, abstract paintings, was a household name. Another of Meconi's influences, the celebrated Mexican architect Luis Barragán, came out of retirement to design Casa Gilardi, a Mexico City masterpiece, around a jacaranda tree. As fate would have it, the nucleus of Meconi's California garden is also a tree, albeit a paperbark.

Like Barragán, Meconi's architectural designs aren't founded on symmetry because he believes it produces static environments. "When the eye focuses on a central axis, it assumes it's looking at two identical halves, so it gets lazy. On the other hand, the eye perceives asymmetry as incomplete, so it's engaged, and its search for resolution amounts to a feeling of spaciousness. There's something satisfying about walking into an asymmetrical space and feeling as if it's activated by your presence. It's as if you are the missing part of a puzzle," he says, explaining a theory he applies to gardens and interiors equally.

His sparsely furnished house and courtyard have an order, simplicity, and understatement characteristic of a Japanese aesthetic, and occasionally he questions whether it's too minimal: "I wondered if paring things down and deaccessorizing stripped the place of its sensuality, but the opposite turns out to be true," he says. "With less clutter, people come here and feel liberated. It's as if there's nothing preventing them from fully inhabiting the space."

The garden appears to be furnished rather than merely planted. White walls, gray gravel, and earth-colored concrete floors inside and out showcase vibrant green, charger-size plant leaves and a colorful collection of midcentury Blenko glass vases that Meconi rotates as if they were seasonal flowers. Mexican feather grass—considered invasive in some places, though it needs constant replacement here—beneath the paperbark tree resembles an overgrown shag carpet.

OPPOSITE Alex Meconi's Venice living room and garden share a continuous, polished concrete floor. Past a paperbark tree (*Melaleuca quinquenervia*), a tall hedge of fern pines (*Afrocarpus gracilior*) runs behind a portable cabinet where Meconi stores surfing equipment.

In the evening, the garden's atmosphere turns sultry as uplighting dramatically silhouettes the paperbark tree and Mexican feather grass (*Nassella tenuissima*).

Prehistoric-looking tree philodendrons growing parallel to a windowsill behind the indoor dining table function as wallpaper and qualify as the ground floor's main form of art. A row of fern pines behind the philodendrons will mature into a hedge. Even when the window is closed, the connection to the garden is manifest.

A pool of water in a living space is exotic in some parts of the world and mundane in others. In California's drought conditions, water is treasured, and in this setting, it is also a source of sound, movement, reflectivity, and sensuality. "Just having it here strategically calms my nerves," says Meconi. At night, when all the interior lamps are turned on, the garden's perimeter lighting silhouettes the paperbark tree and Mexican feather grass and the cantilevered sofa appears to levitate. Under darkness, the house expands out into the garden and the garden returns the favor and retreats inside. ⌄

A 1950s rattan chair and a slatted wooden sofa are the prime pieces of furniture in the exterior living room. At the end of a canal-shaped water feature, Meconi planted five fragrant *Michelia champaca* 'Alba' trees, and he is training creeping fig vine to smother the back wall.

Asymmetry

Traditional designers who tend to favor symmetry place furnishings or plants on either side of a central axis to establish a formal sense of balance, which, according to Meconi, can feel grand and confined at the same time. A preference for asymmetry is associated with a modern sensibility because it's looser and less predictable. Inside and out, asymmetric designs involve odd, not even, numbers. For example, three objects to carry the visual weight on a horizontal surface; a single urn positioned to the right of a doorway instead of one on either side. To Meconi's eyes, mismatched chairs, groupings of dissimilar shrubs, or something slightly off-kilter all feel spontaneous, relaxed, and less rigid than a perfectly balanced, symmetrical arrangement. ⬦

Greenery, including champaca trees, reflects in the living room's side window.

OPPOSITE Thanks to two large picture windows and a sliding wall of glass doors, the living room and the garden are extensions of each other.

SOULFUL SOIL

AT THE AGE OF ELEVEN, MARK RIPEPI'S INTUITIVE UNDERSTANDING of "right plant, right place" led him to transplant a withering young maple tree in his family's Long Island garden. He could have simply moved it to a patch of richer, more irrigated soil, but the young Ripepi had foresight. He envisioned the tree's growth pattern. He saw it eventually providing shade and blocking an unsightly view, so he placed it strategically. He watered it, it thrived, and he was hooked.

Teachers at horticulture school in the mid-1960s routinely dismissed Ripepi's design proposals as overly grand, but post-graduation, he found a mentor in Luther Greene, a flamboyant theatrical producer turned landscape designer. Greene operated out of a chinoiserie- and Delft pottery–filled greenhouse on Sutton Place, in Manhattan. He visited his clients' garden sites dressed in white linen suits and commissioned Salvador Dalí to design his stationery. Over the course of an apprenticeship, Ripepi absorbed Greene's innate horticultural flair, plantsman's eye, and propensity for staging.

After Ripepi launched his own landscaping business, a client's project brought him to New York's Hudson Valley, where he eventually bought six acres and a boarded-up shack. On the day he took ownership of the property, he climbed onto the roof to prove that it was indeed the highest spot for miles around. The iconic garden at Sissinghurst was planned with a pencil, a stack of graph paper, bamboo sticks, and string—and Ripepi used similarly basic tools to design his. But before planting anything, he cleared and terraced the land to bring in the sun and then he bulldozed a back pasture, where he eventually built a stable for his horse.

Echoing the advice of Russell Page, Ripepi's axial layout provides focal direction. On either side of the central lawn, he planted a network of intimate gardens, like rooms off the main corridor of a house. His actual house features more than three dozen windows and multiple doors with immediate access to the outside. In a conventional setup, living room sofas may be oriented toward a fireplace, but in Ripepi's case, they face the gardens outside, which stretch as far as the eye can see because his graduated planting scheme appropriates majestic trees from neighboring properties.

When Ripepi designs a new garden, he adopts another of Page's principles and assesses the dimensional attributes of each tree, shrub, structure, or statue as if it were an object in space. Roberto Burle Marx did something similar when he reduced plants to a color, shape, or volume. Interior designer John Saladino

OPPOSITE In a sunken garden, Ripepi planted a variegated Japanese maple (*Acer palmatum* 'Bloodgood'), wisteria (*Wisteria floribunda*), and topiary boxwood with a carpet of periwinkle as a groundcover.

A lichen-covered urn frames a bucolic sea of greenery in the main garden, including a sheared boxwood hedge and Japanese dogwood (*Cornus kousa* 'Wolf Eyes'), before it directs the gaze to a horizon line of mature trees.

sees it as a painter's technique when he reduces lamps, tables, and chairs to shapes and draws floor plans full of circles, squares, triangles, and rectangles. According to his method, it works for gardens as well, because inside or out we are always walking into a still life.

Hedges are Ripepi's preferred form of structure, but he also uses fences, and his garden rooms follow a processional sequence. A weeping birch begins his visualization of an alfresco vestibule. This area leads to a narrow walkway lined with catmint that culminates in a display of hydrangeas with a creamy coloration as nostalgic as a collection of Wedgwood china. Behind a door is a regimented boxwood arrangement, as linear as a library. In the garden, furniture is sculptural rather than comfortable because Ripepi wants the experience of walking through it to be as ephemeral as the piano music he plays, so he leaves guests to wander, savor the atmosphere, and take it away with them in their mind's eye. ✧

A grassy pathway, enclosed by hedges of yew and rhododendron and lined with beds of blue-flowering catmint, serves as a back corridor between several outdoor rooms.

Pruned and notched boxwood shrubs privatize an outdoor dining area close to the house where Ripepi likes to serve tea in bone china cups.

OPPOSITE "Concentrated, high contrast is crucial whenever a part of a garden is primarily seen from a distance," says Ripepi. "Here, the dark, coarse leaves and rigid pruning of the taxus and holly tonics the loose, variegated dogwood."

As it divides beds of phlox (*Phlox paniculata* 'David') and variegated box elder (*Acer negundo* 'Flamingo'), a rusted gate nestled into a yew hedge functions as the main doorway to the back of the property.

OPPOSITE Ripepi rearranges a set of Adirondack chairs to face the most pleasing views any given season can offer and, into the bargain, he doesn't have to contend with permanent indentations in the lawn.

ABOVE Mark Ripepi laid out several areas in his upstate New York garden as if he were configuring a large mansion. He thinks of a snow-covered weeping birch (*Betula pendula* 'Dalecarlica'), with its necklace of dwarf Japanese barberry, as the rear garden's wintry vestibule.

ABOVE RIGHT Ripepi designed and hand built a stately looking tool shed in between a gray dogwood and a bayberry tree.

In Flux

Like many designers, Mark Ripepi thinks of his own garden as a sort of laboratory, a testing ground for the hardiness of trees, shrubs, and flowers he may eventually recommend to clients, and he has learned to love its perpetual state of flux. Interior designer Michael Taylor, who pioneered the concept of bringing the outdoors inside, was one of the first decorators to leave rooms "in progress." He liked to say, "There is still a place for a painting on that wall, still a chair to be found that will suit that corner. Meanwhile, the room stays alive, young, and growing." Of his own property, Ripepi says, "It's an unfinished, ever-changing undertaking, and as it's deliberately incomplete, it fosters a sense of possibility." ↓

An archway cut into a hemlock
hedge (*Tsuga canadensis*)
surrounding a pond filled with
white waterlilies and sedge
(*Carex elata* 'Knightshayes')
doubles as a shortcut to the
stable where Ripepi boards Tron,
his horse.

POETRY IN MOTION

OPPOSITE In a garden Stuart Towner designed in Winchester, England, yew hedges soften the dominance of the feature wall and reinforce the clean architectural lines of the facing house.

A fractured steel sculpture, created by Johannesburg-based artist Regardt van der Meulen, helps to demarcate the garden before the grade slopes precipitously.

THE DRAMATIC FOCAL POINT OF THE GARDEN Stuart Towner designed in Winchester, England, is a visual verse: a steel rendering of an imaginary wind scattering a life-size woman into leaves. Inside the house, another lyrical gesture, an eighty-year old olive tree, commands a sky-lit glass-enclosed courtyard adjacent to the living room designed by architects at AR Design Studio. The apparent role reversals—a sculpture of a person who is at one with nature and a domesticated tree planted inside a vitrine—are appropriate given the house's inverted space planning.

Similar to properties taking advantage of beach or ocean views, the home's bedrooms are on the ground floor, while its entrance hall, living room, dining room, and kitchen are upstairs. Like traditional French parterres, Towner's landscape is meant to be primarily appreciated from above. Thanks to an expanse of windows and glass rails around a large balcony, the top floor of the house takes in an unobstructed vista of sky, garden, sculpture, historic church spires, and a distant national park. Towner knew the garden could never detract from views this breathtaking, just as he knew that his garden couldn't compete with the house's strong geometry. His intuition was to keep things simple. When he began to draw up a plan, he decided to make few brushstrokes—all of them deliberate, and one or two of them grand.

At the garden level, where a cantilevered roof already shaded a dining terrace, Towner extended the floor and installed limestone pavers that morph into a wide staircase and lead to a stepped seating area around a sunken fire pit.

Beyond the hardscape, an expanse of lawn, his largest gesture, stops short of a proscenium-like wall where the regal sculpture stands. For Towner, the sea of green mirrored the house's mass and gave the statement architecture space to breathe. As the grass is mown diagonally, it resembles a living room's wall-to-wall, broad-striped carpet. Long pathways and low yew hedges border the lawn on both sides, and in certain light, their axial alignment renders the garden as a drop-shadow of the house. The feature wall's rectangular window functions like a camera's viewfinder, aimed to capture the property's central axis. From the front side, it frames a canopy of two multistemmed juneberry (*Amelanchier lamarckii*) trees. From behind, it focuses on the horizontality and transparency of the light-filled house.

As he does in every garden he designs, Towner took into account the house's proportions, and here he also keyed off the architecture's materials and colors. The extensive interior brickwork found its way onto stair risers,

low retaining walls, and planters filled with rough horsetails, whose tiny dark brown bands mimic the cedar siding. The brick's gray color echoes the internal doors and porcelain flooring and, in a heavily pigmented iteration, it repeats on the garden's feature wall.

The perimeter's mix of silverberry and yew hedges shows seasonal changes. The blooms on echinacea, foxgloves, and bearded irises come and go, but their decaying stems and seed heads survive until midwinter, as seams in the dried grasses turn a shade of golden brown and integrate the house and garden into the greater landscape. ↯

In Towner's reinvention of the lower terrace, the dining area appears to float above the expanse of lawn, allowing diners to take in the tops of silverberry hedges, yew columns, and a tool shed's sedum roof at eye level.

Architectural firm AR Design Studio designed and built what they refer to as an upside-down house. By extending its lower terrace and thereby enlarging the outdoor dining and kitchen areas, Towner made the garden more immediate and all but eliminated any indoor/outdoor distinction.

Brick planters filled
with rough horsetails
(*Equisetum hyemale*)
flanking the sunken
seating area function as
permeable walls.

OPPOSITE On the first
floor of the house,
the architects built
a glass-enclosed
courtyard with sliding
doors for a solitary
olive tree.

Listening

Interior designer Lella Vignelli once said, "I listen to what the space says—the walls, the windows. You can't change what that space wants to be." In the Winchester garden he designed, Stuart Towner applied the same principle and was guided by his clients' love of minimalism, by the house's architecture, and by its environs. Once he discovered what the garden aspired to be, he lifted materials and a color palette from the existing brickwork, exterior cladding, flooring, and doors, which he echoed in the textures of the plantings. As a result, the garden looks and feels in tandem with the house. ✥

STRUCTURE

WITHOUT STRUCTURE, A GARDEN IS MERELY AN OPEN FIELD. It may have layered beds with tall, hierarchal plantings or waist-high rows of grass to create verticality, but without some kind of permanent organizational framework, there's nothing to focus on, nothing to anchor the viewer's eye. There's nowhere for a plant to climb, no hideaway, no transition, nothing to deflect wind or muffle sound, no gate to enter, and nothing to reach at the end of a pathway. There's nothing to block an unsightly view or frame a beautiful one. No stops and starts, beginnings or ends. Without structure, without bones, there's no opportunity for a garden or a room to be whimsical, grand, intimate, or serene, because it has no character. Too little structure and there's no "there" there—nowhere to hang a proverbial hat; it looks as if nobody's home.

The subtext of an erect line is permanence, formality, stability, and dignity, and any vertical element ranks as a perpendicular resistance to Earth's gravitational pull. When structure is used for its own sake, it can produce a feeling of chaos, which, in interior design and landscaping terms, translates to claustrophobia. A design with too many vertical lines has the same effect as a string of punctuation marks in a sentence. It's equivalent to a command to stay at attention or to sit with a straight back. Perhaps the test for gauging just the right amount of verticality is whether a garden still piques our interest during the winter, when structure is all that remains.

The surfaces of a floor, the lowest horizontal plane of a room or garden, should recede and support all the other surfaces. As decorator Billy Baldwin often said, you never want the ground to jump up and say hello. When we're outside, different floor surfaces affect how we walk. Slate pavers let us glide, cobblestones produce an awkward gait, uneven boulders make us wary, sand slows us down, and moss makes us tiptoe. Ideally, garden pathways are broader than those inside, wide enough to accommodate two people walking side by side.

The higher horizontal plane of a ceiling, pergola, or arbor is settling. It contributes a sense of calm, reassurance, stability, repose, and tranquility (Baldwin found ceilings to be the most neglected part of a room and referred to them as a sixth wall). Vertical lines are likely to be more present in a small garden or an apartment, while horizontal lines figure prominently in large interior spaces or in rural gardens.

In landscape design, the law of significant enclosure, based on behavioral psychology, articulates a state of spatial balance as a 3:1 ratio between all the horizontal and vertical structures and is a reminder that all upright, level, and ground planes are aspects of a holistic composition. In the right proportion, they make us feel comfortable and safe.

A tree ranks as a garden's supreme form of structure. A tall birch draws the eye up and elevates the spirit. A generous oak provides shade and shelter, screens out an unsightly view, visually links the sky and land, and creates a habitat for birds and other creatures. For these reasons and more, a designer may advise a client with a limited budget to look on a tree as a structural investment and a mutable piece of sculpture no matter whether its habit is rounded, fastigiate, or spreading. ✦

OPPOSITE At the Madoo Conservancy in Sagaponack, New York, pleached and shaped hornbeams create a generous, coved ceiling above an intimate dining area.

BELOW, FROM LEFT TO RIGHT:

In Carl D'Aquino's upstate New York garden, a low, running dry-stacked stone wall is punctuated with an urn full of begonias.

Landscape designer Dean Riddle likes to attach ash and hemlock saplings to hemlock posts in the organic fences he creates.

Mown grass demarcates a roomlike area immediately around a small, lone maple and allows it to carry the visual weight of an entire field.

HEDGING BETS

AS BUILDERS ADDED THE FINAL DETAILING to his Greek Revival farmhouse in New York's Hudson Valley, Brian McCarthy was envisioning its garden, as he had done for several months. Newly carved out of sixteen acres of alfalfa fields, it was a level, blank canvas, and his sketchbook was full of drawings of paths, hedges, flower beds, trees, lotus ponds, and pavilions. By the time he and his partner, Daniel Sagar, moved in, with nothing more than a collapsible card table, the garden's concept was set.

As an interior designer, McCarthy creates room skylines—dynamic routes for the eye to travel around furniture silhouettes and touch down on stimulating objects and art—and he imagined his garden the same way. As with a room, structure was the first consideration. With the collaboration of landscape designer Marge Brower, McCarthy set up a symmetrical courtyard at the front of the house, with hydrangeas framed by waves of clipped boxwoods, a design vocabulary he continued to repeat prolifically. On the land's perimeter, he interspersed forsythia in between maples, pin oaks, and spruce, which were around 8 feet tall at the time—a decade later, they are close to three times that height. Brower's crew planted more than 1,000 hornbeam whips along 600 linear feet, and today 9-foot-tall L-shaped hedges protect at least half the garden.

McCarthy's brimming beds adhere to Vita Sackville-West's general approach to planting: "profusion, even extravagance and exuberance, within confines of the utmost linear severity." One of his favorite combinations is dogwood, catmint, and tall grasses, with a submissive edging of lady's mantle. "Undulating borders always feel as if they have age and a sense of place," he says, "especially in a newly established garden, where plants can sometimes feel a bit *Wizard of Oz*, as if they'd fallen straight from the sky."

The garden's semiformality is a match for the house's semigrandeur. The living room's 10-foot-high ceiling is generous enough for oversize paintings and sizable antiques, and its width easily accommodates several sofas around a central fireplace. As McCarthy designed the garden, he kept in mind how it would look from inside the house and from an attached porch, and those vantage points are integral to his scheme.

Like all expansive interiors, McCarthy's garden offers immediate and distant focal points. At a back entrance, a large rusted urn at the center of an axial path guides guests ahead to the porch on the left or the pool pavilion on the right. "I put in a few functional gates, but even though there are no actual doorways, there's a reoccurring experience of opening and enclosing as you walk about,"

OPPOSITE In Brian McCarthy and Daniel Sagar's upstate New York garden, the fall showing of various miscanthus and pennisetum grasses, shrubs, and trees surrounding the porch match the texture and coloration of its furnishings.

Hydrangeas (*Hydrangea arborescens* 'Annabelle') and giant allium seed heads epitomize the color palette and textural range of the plantings as well as the house's décor.

he says. "There's always something to lure the eye onward. Inside or out, the aim is to walk through a space and be arrested by shape, proportion, texture, juxtaposition, and color, followed by breathing room."

After generations of producing alfalfa, the meadow still encroaches on the garden and will do so for as long as birds recycle their seeds. "For some reason, I never thought about birds when I was mapping everything out," says McCarthy. "But once the first large tree was firmly in the ground, they came immediately. I mean, flocks of them! And it was a magical moment. Creating a habitat for them is a wonderful, unplanned bonus." ⌄

CLOCKWISE, FROM TOP:

Close to a pond, boxwood hedges, rounded clumps of grasses, sprawling butterfly bush, dogwoods, and hydrangeas form a beautiful hierarchy of vibrant greenery.

Giant allium seed heads repeatedly emerge from beds of emerald-colored grass alongside several of the garden's meandering pathways.

A tightly clipped boxwood serpentines around an ornamental cherry tree.

Globe-shaped finials on a low, bluestone wall echo the border of boxwood balls that line the long entry to the main house.

Boxwood, viburnum, and hydrangea repeated throughout the garden create one of the overtones in its rhythmic voice.

OPPOSITE A hornbeam hedge stabilizes a crop of *Miscanthus sinensis* 'Variegatus' at the base of an ornamental cherry tree.

Layers of grasses, hydrangeas, and a hornbeam hedge are contained by a thick row of lady's mantle.

FROM LEFT TO RIGHT:

Midwinter strips a hornbeam hedge and high mounds of *Miscanthus sinensis* 'Adagio' of their color, but heightens their tactility.

Once all the surrounding foliage scrolls through every conceivable fall color, the hardy hornbeam begins to lose its vibrancy.

Even in the dead of winter, boxwood, spruce, and red twig dogwood (*Cornus alba* 'Ivory Halo') retain their structural presence.

OPPOSITE As if balancing the layering in the garden's tightly planted beds, an armillary sphere mounted on an ornate pedestal is framed by dry-stacked walls and hornbeam hedges as it directs the eye to neighboring farmland and distant views of mountains.

RIGHT The end of a row of crabapple trees is punctuated by a boxwood-encircled antique armillary sphere.

BELOW RIGHT An oversized urn surrounded with swaths of hydrangeas, grasses, and lady's mantle and positioned at the convergence of two paths helps to direct circulation.

Shape

From an aerial view, the layout of Brian McCarthy's garden looks formal—a series of rectangles and squares, with several lines indicating long, straight stretches of hedges surrounding a circular lily pond. Strolling through the garden, however, it seems more relaxed, because softer shapes echo the water feature's curvaceous edge. Close-planted boxwoods form running borders, and their spherical shapes repeat in globelike ornaments flanking a pathway, in vibrant allium balls, and in the plump Annabelle hydrangeas. In an interior space, circles feel embracing and playful; here, within the garden's linear framework, they come across as balanced, contained movement. They also demonstrate the importance of creating rooms, inside or outside, with a dynamic mix of geometry. ❧

OUTSIDE THE BOX

ANYONE FAMILIAR WITH THE HISTORY OF TUUSULA, a Finnish lake district twenty miles outside Helsinki, may look at the full-throated terraces Sari Lampinen designed in a garden there and wonder whether their color and abundance is a nod to the region's romantic past, when its shores and picturesque landscapes attracted renowned poets, composers, and painters. They may also speculate that her simple, rectilinear pavilion references some aspect of the region's even earlier industrial past. In fact, Lampinen's design is anything but nostalgic. It was dictated by the site, the soil, the weather, and her clients' needs.

Marrying modernism and romanticism is a staple of Lampinen's design firm, Puksipuu, just as it's characteristic of the gardens produced by her strongest influence, Swedish landscape architect Ulf Nordfjell. Lampinen's knowledge of plant communities comes from her admiration of Pentti Alanko, one of Finland's top botanists, and she inherited her love of exuberant, close planting from Irish plant hunter Jimi Blake, who taught her to be partial to long-blooming perennials that prolong a garden's peaking time.

The pavilion looks elemental enough to be portable, when in fact its slatted framework is firmly fixed in place. If a view defines a building's character, then based on its nearby fields, forests, and waterways, the pavilion is truly gallant. It's also obligingly utilitarian. It offers privacy from neighbors, which is its raison d'être—yet its slim silhouette still affords the main house visual access to a distant lake. An attached awning cools off its Siberian larch patio on hot summer days, and a wood-burning stove heats its snug interior in colder weather.

As a piece of pure geometry, the pavilion is a muted backdrop for a cornucopia of plants, and its gray exterior reflects the color scheme inside the property's main house. The living room's printed curtains and nubby pillows inspired the ornamental natural mulches and rough stone surfaces of the hardscaping, as well as the burgundy-striped, spiky blades of cordyline, clusters of stonecrop, and wisps of foxtail grass. Steps supply more geometry and delineate beds containing shapely juxtapositions of round and pointed leaves, flowers, and needles that sprout, trail, feather, bristle, and droop in a painterly manner.

All interior designers and landscapers understand the value of highlighting certain views and disguising others; here, one wall of the pavilion has no openings, while sliding glass doors frame a purple-leafed, weeping apple tree and a silver spruce. A seat by the fire focuses on a long, narrow window that glances onto a small rhododendron, a grove of junipers, and the distant landscape. ⌄

OPPOSITE In a Finnish garden, Sari Lampinen designed a pavilion where large glass windows take in views of a lake and nearby fields. Her dense, richly colored planting scheme includes European boxwood, Swiss mountain pine, and cinquefoil (*Sibbaldiopsis tridentata* 'Nuuk') and complements planters filled with blue fescue.

Potted topiaries change according to season, as do the interior accessories.

Thick groundcovers, including Siberian carpet cypress (*Microbiota decussata*), cinquefoil, stonecrop, lady's mantle, and Swiss mountain pine soften the edges of an angular retaining wall.

BELOW, FROM LEFT TO RIGHT:

Planters overflowing with pruned Monterey cypress (*Cupressus macrocarpa* 'Goldcrest') and trailing variegated ivy spend winters in a cool, underground cellar.

A screen of junipers and a bed closely planted with boxwood, stonecrop, and plantain lilies encircles the dining patio as potted chrysanthemums decorate the table.

Repeats of purple—such as this variety of sweet basil—contribute to the garden's visual rhythm.

OPPOSITE Over time, a hedge of *Thuja occidentalis* 'Smaragd' will develop enough to screen the far side of the pavilion and provide more privacy. A wood stove, lanterns, and candles draped with twigs from a black chokeberry hedge illuminate the pavilion at night.

Suitability

Lampinen's pavilion is as functional and unpretentious as a potting shed. Without the wood-burning stove, it would serve only as a summer house; if it were purely for show, it might qualify as a folly. As is, it nestles into its immediate and greater surroundings; it is totally born from the site and meant to be comfortably occupied in all four seasons. The contrast between the abundantly full beds of plants and the pavilion's linear bone structure is comparable to a richly floral suzani textile coming alive in a sparsely furnished room. Knowing when to go for abundance, as Lampinen did with her intimate plantings, and when to hold back, as she did with the restrained piece of architecture, are both important aspects of spatial design. ✦

SHEAR GENIUS

THE WELL-PRUNED, THIRTEEN-ACRE CONNECTICUT PROPERTY Robert Couturier shares with Jeffrey Morgan, a historic preservationist, was once an abandoned hemlock forest. In its current incarnation, it's easy to imagine its topiaries, parterres, woodlands, allées, avenues of yews, and lilacs as characters in an Alice in Wonderland–meets–Edward Scissorhands movie, directed by Peter Greenaway.

Couturier, an interior designer, planned to build a small pavilion directly after he acquired the land in the early 2000s. To make room, he cut down a few pines days before an intense storm destroyed a remaining grove, upending trees and exposing their massive roots. "The disaster had its bright side," he says, "because I wouldn't have had the heart to cut them down. They were so mature. But immediately we had light, followed soon after by swarms of birds and bees." His humble pavilion concept morphed into a much larger and "vaguely European" residence, and the size of the garden mushroomed in parallel.

Couturier tells his clients that houses and gardens should reflect who their owners actually are, as opposed to who they think they need to be. It's a philosophy he readily practices, which is why, as someone who is both highly mannered and gregarious, his precisely trimmed hedges are a stone's throw away from wild-looking fields of ferns, lilacs, and viburnum. It's also why the house's baronial interior is a fun, hospitable, and relaxing place to visit.

Outside, a similar intimacy stems from drama, monumental scale, uniformity of color, and a sense of play. A walk in and about the manicured gardens at Versailles was once described as a "peaceful pursuit of happiness," and the proportional harmony of Couturier's garden feels the same, thanks to his gardener, Clive Lodge. A long stroll past giant boxwood spheres, angular pyramids, a perfect circle of arborvitae, and a rock garden approached by a giant, mulched stairway all have joyride potential. On weekends, Couturier strolls his property, with his five shih tzus in tow, a few times each day. His preference to be either completely outdoors or snug inside the house is why no intermediary terraces, loggias, or porches exist.

Neither are there benches placed along the way for reflection, even though many striking vignettes pop up every few feet. Walking slowly through the garden, visitors can't help but notice the spatial relationships between the hedges and an axial allée. At dawn and dusk, the entire garden takes on an alter ego, when shadowy perceptions between real and unreal are likely to play visual

OPPOSITE A Louis XV table and Jacob fauteuils of the same period sit on a limestone floor in the entry hall in Robert Couturier's house in Kent, Connecticut. An oversize, copper-framed mirror marks and reflects the transition between his well-pruned garden and the house's stately interior.

At dusk, the box-pruned hornbeams (*Carpinus betulus*) in the rectangular allée drop dramatic shadows and take on a majestic surreality.

tricks. Standing still, observing the garden's heightened stillness just after dawn is particularly rewarding—in misty light, a spider's cobweb stretched across a flat plane of boxwood resembles a gossamer handkerchief.

The seasons have little effect on the interior furnishings: the spring and summer draperies have no cold-weather equivalents, and carpets stay in place year after year. Preparing the garden for winter, however, is an involved process: All the boxwood is wrapped to insulate it from January's snow and biting winds. Dozens of planters are shipped off to a greenhouse to be brought out again in early spring, when they're filled with snapdragons and pansies. "The garden may look monumental and robust," says Couturier, "but it's also delicate and sensitive. A late frost, an early snowfall, an extended drought, or a sudden cold snap can be ruinous and heartbreaking, but then spring comes and all is right with the world." ⚶

In the lower boxwood garden, long, angular hedges disguise a bluestone stairway that leads to the hornbeam allée.

Centuries-old, carved marble vessels dispersed throughout the property establish circulation routes in much the same way as strategic placements of furniture do inside the house. In the parterre, metal urns filled with fan flowers (*Scaevola aemula*) are under-planted with a robust collar of lady's mantle.

Perfectly pruned boxwood orbs punctuate and emphasize corners of the parallel hedges in the parterre.

OPPOSITE Gently undulating hedges in the lower boxwood garden are trimmed to avoid interfering with the layered architecture of the house as well as long, overall views of the surrounding landscape.

In the lower garden, an arrangement of bronze ginkgo-shaped furniture is more sculptural than practical. Its rounded, organic edges contrast with a pyramidal-pruned box and an upright column of arborvitae.

A gilded French Louis XV daybed is positioned
to absorb the afternoon sun that streams
through a window on the second floor, which
captures a view of a pond.

Rounded boxwoods flank each entrance to a circular arborvitae "room," where Couturier placed an urn at center stage.

From the parterre overlook, a grass-carpeted pathway is edged by white-flowering viburnum (*Viburnum tomentosum*), showy stonecrop (*Hylotelephium spectabile*), Jacob's ladder (*Polemonium*), and common pink (*Dianthus plumarius*).

Scale and Proportion

In most of our homes, we've standardized the dimensions for counter and table heights, door and hall widths. We're instantly oriented every time we reach for a door handle or a light switch, because it's placed at our convenience. Outdoors, the sky is literally the limit, so establishing relatable proportions is crucial, especially in a monumentally scaled garden. Robert Couturier's placement of pots and urns throughout his property humanizes a 20-foot-tall hedge or a long allée. The size variance is animating, because uniform scale, even when it's larger than life—as it is in Couturier's garden—can feel static. Experimenting with proportion—weighing and contrasting the relative sizes of objects—produces the richest gardens and the most dynamic interiors. ✦

A family of late-nineteenth-century figurines defines the exterior wall of the dining room.

COURT IN THE ACT

DURING ONE OF HIS FIRST VISITS TO A COURTYARD he was commissioned to redesign in the British town of Newmarket, in Suffolk, Hugo Nicole remembers the vibrant leaves of a Japanese maple at its glorious peak. He knew the tree would have to stay in place, as would several stretches of weathered, craggy brick walls. He also planned to retain some swagged, trailing roses around a pool, working them into his new design by installing geometric pavers nearby. He knew their clean lines would take the saccharine out of the Victorian concept the way a modernist sofa's frame takes the granny out of chintz upholstery.

Any garden, like any interior, is best when it includes a range of materials, and the predominance of brickwork here could have been too much of a good thing if Nicole hadn't balanced and subdued it in a number of ways. For example, he planted an espaliered crabapple screen perpendicular to the longest wall to break up its continuous line, and clipped yew sentinels now soften the frameworks of a dozen brick doorways.

Nicole's design sensibility is influenced by iconic English gardens such as Hidcote, Sissinghurst, and Great Dixter, as well as the tapestried Mediterranean garden Nicole de Vésian created in Provence. A textile designer, de Vésian used round shapes to craft her garden's flow and rhythm. Nicole did the same in an anteroom at one end of the Newmarket courtyard, where he balanced the angular structure with circles and globes. He installed a raised plinth around a central water feature, an acrylic sphere filled with water overflowing into a dish—a sort of fountain the artist Allison Armour refers to as an "aqualens." Its planted border contains several sheared boxwood spheres and two varieties of late-flowering allium.

Nicole also took a sensual approach by transforming a walled garden room into an aromatherapist's dream, with a perfumer's haul of fragrant blooms, including lily of the valley, sweet box, wintersweet, honeysuckle, shrub rose, cyclamen, rosemary, clematis, thyme, European sage, and verbena. As a sensorial tease, a textural bed directly outside the room is filled with euphorbia, burnet, ceanothus, and climbing roses.

His treatment of the hardscaping is more subliminal. Close to the base of the house, in the section where a back hall, breakfast area, and drawing room face the courtyard, he laid rough-hewn Yorkstone pavers—bargaining that their aged appearance was close enough in era to the Georgian house's architecture. Leading away toward a newer pool court, he laid flat-sawn pavers with cleaner lines. Both cuts of stone are of the same hue, but each interacts differently with

OPPOSITE A brick-walled courtyard designed by Hugo Nicole in Newmarket, England, features strategically planted shrubs in the brick wall to soften all the doorways' lines. He chose groundcovers such as lady's mantle (*Alchemilla mollis*) and fleabane (*Erigeron karvinkianus*) that spill over onto pathways.

Ringed by two types of allium (*Allium hollandicum* 'Purple Sensation' and *A. sphaerocephalon*), a central, acrylic sphere circulating water until it overflows into a dish is a conceptual take on a conventional water feature.

light. When he inserted long strips of Belgian pavers into the Yorkstone, he envisioned an interior designer dispersing kilims across a wooden floor.

Come spring, the brick walls' rusty red is interrupted by the pristine colors of early anemone and tulip bulbs. Soon afterward, the parasol ornamental pears and crabapples begin to flower before other plants have even sprouted their leaves. Next comes the euphorbia, and soon after, a blooming continuum of perennials and roses, agapanthus and lavender. Some day, all the brick walls will be curtained with living floral fabric. ⤵

To amplify the courtyard's angular lines, Nicole underplanted pleached Callary pear trees (*Pyrus calleryana* 'Chanticleer') with squared boxwood and placed a rectangular (rather than round) table on the central axis.

OPPOSITE A Japanese maple
shades an espaliered screen
of crabapple trees that will
ultimately transform into a
dense, fragrant room divider.

RIGHT Given a few more
seasons, climbing roses will
flesh out and surround a
newly created opening to
the fragrance garden and
dining area.

BELOW Purple grapevines
trained to camouflage the
side of a wall opening that
looks onto the courtyard
and house pick up on the
brickwork's deeper tones.

Deep beds around the pool are densely planted with a hierarchy of purple-red flowers, including agapanthus, echinacea, lamb's ears, Cape honeysuckle, allium, euphorbia, vervain, and catnip.

OPPOSITE A new opening between the fragrant garden and the pool looks onto an orderly row of box-formed hornbeams.

Framing

Highlighting and disguising are basic parts of any design process, and, as any artist or photographer knows, once you mount something inside a frame, whether it's a wrinkled piece of paper or a Picasso drawing, it acquires a certain importance. A doorway or window is an architectural frame, but the concept of directing the eye to a particular view or vignette doesn't necessarily involve structure. It's also a mindset—a way of perceiving a garden or an interior as if it's a series of visual experiences. It involves careful planting or furnishing to edit the superfluous so every focal point is contained and unencumbered. It's a controlled, momentary way of "seeing the forest for the trees" before taking in and appreciating all the possibilities the whole encompasses. ↴

MOVEMENT

SITTING DOWN OR STANDING STILL is invariably the best way to appreciate a living room, to tune into its sounds, weigh up the shape of its objects, and evaluate its textures and colors. When we view a painting or a piece of sculpture, we tend to study it from a few different perspectives in order to determine its best angle. That's also the way we savor a garden. As we walk, a garden's narrative unfolds and we tune into its rhythm. As we stroll, we digest all the nuances of its personality, and its textures, fragrances, and colors take on form and dimension. From a design perspective, the most animated garden may have an angular superstructure, but it more than likely has a subtext or overlay of circles, arcs, loops, curls, ellipses, and waves.

Plants grow toward the sun, although some may trail off as they climb a trellis—perhaps toward a water source? When we are left to our own devices, we rarely walk in a straight line; like a vining plant, we tend to wander. A meandering path slows our pace, invites a lingering pause; a winding or circular path gives us an opportunity to stop and smell the primroses. Inside a house, whenever an architect incorporates a spiral staircase, she wants to save time and economize space; but outside, when a spiral is the foundational shape of a labyrinth or maze, it has an opposite significance and facilitates an expansive, meditative journey.

Gardens and interiors share a lexicon of styles, including midcentury modern, cottage, minimalist, Zen, traditional, and French formal, some of which are based on man-made symmetry, while others mimic nature's curvaceous, graceful flow. If shapes have personalities, an angle is serious, formal, and unbending, while a curve is lighthearted, informal, and adaptable. Inside, a few curves can take the seriousness out of a room full of square windows and rectangular doors; outside, they can lighten up a geometrical flower bed and save it from appearing static. When they're not used sparingly or purposefully, curves fall into the decorative category and sometimes they rank as mere embellishment. Ornamentally, they're associated with curtain swags, curlicues, and scrolls, and in excess, they tend to come across as busy, fussy, and superfluous.

Whenever a curve breathes air into a small area (imagine a half-moon sink in a cramped bathroom, a serpentine-shaped sofa in a small sitting room, an undulating hedge, or a shapely urn softening a cornered recess in a yard), it provides the illusion of space. A well-defined curve is equally strong and soft and the mind tends to imagine it complete and transformed into a circle, symbolizing protection and completion. An angular chair may satisfy the intellect, but a chair with a rounded back and plump upholstery promises and delivers comfort.

Duplications of a color in a garden are rhythmic and can be dramatic, particularly when the same plant specimen is used en masse, but even more so when the whole configures into a curve or an undulating wave. Nature doesn't abhor a straight line—it's just more in favor of the shapelier kind. ⬇

OPPOSITE An elliptical sofa in Richard Silverstein's Los Angeles house humanizes the modernist architecture's angularity and encourages the eye to wander outside into the hilly landscape.

BELOW, FROM LEFT TO RIGHT:

Water concentrically swirling in a stone-lined stream introduces sound and motion to a momentarily captured shaft of light.

A spiral topiary mimics the curved base of a flight of stairs and silently indicates the quickest way to exit an Italianate-style garden.

By encircling it with an arbor of trumpet vine, landscape architect Janice Parker gave a pedestaled urn some lyrical gravitas.

AS THE CROW FLIES

OPPOSITE On this sunny patio surrounded by textural plantings in a San Marino garden designed by Judy Kameon, an L-shaped sofa in the outdoor living room adjacent to the house is configured around a mounted fire pit.

A ceramic sculpture by Stan Edmonson is discreetly tucked within the border's plantings beneath a colorful maple (*Acer palmatum* 'Bloodgood').

A MODERNIST 1954 POST-AND-BEAM HOUSE in San Marino, California, sits high up in a shallow valley overlooking a scattering of buildings, including a pool cabana and a guest cottage. When designer Judy Kameon, the principal of Elysian Landscapes, first viewed the site, none of the buildings felt related, and some felt neglected, so she developed a network of interconnecting pathways, a visual language for circulation that lets more of the land be traversed and appreciated.

On the primary routes, such as the path from the house to a ceramics studio, she laid hand-finished concrete. The secondary, more meandering, paths utilize cast-in-place concrete pavers. and compacted decomposed granite covers the rustic, tertiary lanes that venture into the property's outer reaches. In other words, richer materials for heavily trafficked areas, humbler materials for the least traveled. Architects often use a similar type of hierarchy in, let's say, an apartment building by installing terrazzo or pouring concrete floors in a public lobby and laying carpet in a private area such as a residential hall. The former is functional, noisy, and fast-paced, to encourage people to keep moving; the latter is more dignified and comfortable, for a more relaxed tread.

Kameon's plant palette—blue sages, several agave cultivars, aeoniums, lots of grasses, and dense groundcovers—integrates the garden with a series of California live oaks and a mix of variously shaped native, Mediterranean, and subtropical species. She was determined to transform a sad area close to the house into something enchanting, so she set up a dining table and chairs under an umbrella and planted edibles in adjacent raised beds. Because vegetable gardens have fallow periods, Kameon enlivened its borders with plants known to attract hummingbirds, such as kangaroo paw (*Anigozanthos flavidus* 'Orange Cross'), African geranium (*Pelargonium sidoides*), fragrant Grosso lavender (*Lavandula ×intermedia* 'Grosso'), and clumps of *Aloe* 'Cynthia Giddy'. Now the beautiful outdoor dining space upstages its interior counterpart; as her clients literally walk through it en route to the main house, it welcomes them home.

Kameon has a preference for outdoor furniture with patterned upholstery, which is more forgiving to wear and stains than solid fabric. The graphic sofas and chairs outside—she designed them all for her company, Plain Air—complement the playful interior décor, where an immense blue sofa holds court in the living room and the kitchen cabinets hopscotch between orange, aqua, and lime. Inside, the furniture silhouettes are generally kept below sill levels, so nothing interrupts a clear view to the garden. The outdoor sofas and ottomans are similarly streamlined to maintain the open sightlines throughout the now cohesive landscape. ⌄

PREVIOUS SPREAD Sliding glass doors help to obliterate the distinction between the garden and a pool room designed by architects Fung+Blatt. A Spun chair by Heatherwick Studio, a midcentury table, and chairs are all akin to Plain Air's sleek outdoor furniture.

LEFT A rustic path winding through the lowest part of the property was built up with compacted decomposed granite and bordered by silverthorn, acanthus, and lilyturf.

ABOVE Pineapple sage (*Salvia elegans*) flowers contrast with spiny wild rye grass (*Leymus condensatus*) on either side of the hand-finished concrete primary path as it bypasses a California live oak en route to the back garden.

OPPOSITE A concrete retaining wall by the pool doubles as the back of a cantilevered sofa, which is surrounded with blue foxtail agave (*Agave attenuata* 'Nova') and juniper under the shade of a California live oak.

Raised vegetable beds next to the main outdoor eating area provide a "garden-to-table" experience.

OPPOSITE Shaded by a California live oak and a salmon-colored umbrella, and bordered by a variety of grasses, the main outdoor dining room is situated at the back of the house in what was formerly the service entrance.

LEFT Plantings of lavender, agave, and fountain grass achieve abstractions of form and texture.

BELOW LEFT Along a paved, secondary path, Kameon mixed native and Mediterranean subtropical plants, including pineapple sage, *Agave attenuata*, and *Aeonium* 'Carol', where they could soak up the sun.

OPPOSITE Midcentury, abstract pour paintings by Helen Frankenthaler and Morris Louis inspired the swirling pattern of sedums in Kameon's design of the garage roof.

Informality

Kameon devised an orderly way to navigate this San Marino garden, but another challenge was how to best activate all the landings that punctuated the new paths. Her solution was to overlay her well-planned arrangement with adaptable, multi-functional spaces where people can relax, dine, and appreciate all the succulents, vines, flowers, and fruit trees. She also installed lightweight, easily transportable furniture in each living space. Every area has a primary purpose while still maintaining flexibility. Nothing is fixed and formal. ❧

A PATH OF LEAST RESISTANCE

THE ANTICS OF COCO, A WHEATON TERRIER, played an active role when Barbara Samitier designed a garden in Peckham, South London. When the ever-energetic dog spots a fox, a squirrel, or a neighbor's cat, she tends to treat precious shrubs as launching and landing pads. Before Samitier set to work, she traced the dog's "desire line," and along that route, she planted deterrents—spiky, strappy, leathery plants, including Japanese forest grass, New Zealand flax, and lilyturf. In a couple of Coco's frequented haunts, where she liked to tunnel, there are now heavy, immovable pots.

The garden is attached to a four-storied, early Georgian house, where characterful interiors marry a mix of antiques, contemporary furniture, with a collection of contemporary art. An open kitchen and dining room with dark walls and concrete floors have stackable glass doors, so meals are prepared and eaten with trees and plants as a backdrop. Thanks to Samitier, the kitchen is now sandwiched between two living rooms—one indoors, one outside.

In the alfresco room, a weed-free, water-saving porcelain floor covers up the site of a former lawn. Each of its 40-inch square tiles is embossed with a threadbare pattern so it resembles an oft-trodden ancient site. (If Coco misses being able to dig up her old turf, she has so far kept it to herself.) An L-shaped sectional sofa anchors the space and a perimeter of black bamboo functions as its three-dimensional wallpaper. An oversize version of an iconic 1930s Anglepoise lamp amplifies the surreality. Its gray metal finish and the sofa's slate-colored weatherproof upholstery are neutral to avoid upstaging the bright foliage colors.

Samitier completely replanted the area around an existing ash and a colorful cordyline with strong structural evergreen plantings so the garden stays lush and green year-round. Low-maintenance herbaceous plants and flowers are backed by scrims of ginger lilies, verbenas, torch lilies, foxtail lilies, salvias, and sedums. Fragrance comes from *Akebia quinata* and star jasmine vines, as groundcovers form a tightly packed, evergreen carpet.

OPPOSITE In Barbara Samitier's South London design, a sectional sofa defines an outdoor living room. A hedge of black bamboo (*Phyllostachys nigra*) serves as a wall and its depth of color harkens to textiles inside the house.

Hakone grass, the spiked leaves of New Zealand flax, densely planted bugle-weed, Platt's black grass (*Phormium* 'Platt's Black'), and hardy, rubbery mounds of baby's tears (*Soleirolia soleirolii*) all make Coco think twice about burrowing.

Focal points, surprises, and orchestrated views open, close, entice, and draw the eye in. The end of the path that winds its way through the garden isn't visible, so there's a suggested continuance. A brick wall with a small entrance hints at a room behind, even though it's not actually seen. A Buddha head nestled between ferns prompts a momentary pause whenever it is spotted.

To balance the L-shaped sofa and angular tile work, and maybe to commemorate Coco's sporty behavior, several of Samitier's design choices amplify a sense of motion. Swaying bamboos, ornamental grasses, and large-leafed plants such as New Zealand flax, palms, and cycads interact with breezes, as do the leaves of the Japanese maple and birch. Recycled granite paving stones form a curved path. A chair shaped like a Möbius strip in an everlasting loop doubles as a piece of sculpture. A hung mirror reflects subtle changes in the weather and the momentary quirks of the wind, sun, rain, and, occasionally, Coco, as she is about to leap into the air. ⇟

Most of the rectangular garden is taken up by an al fresco living room where walls of black bamboo screening the room's longer sides are strategically interspersed with grasses and spiny yuccas.

LEFT Just like many interior designers, Samatier thinks of a mirror as a device to open up and amplify space, to capture movement and reflect light.

BELOW LEFT Distressed-looking porcelain tiles with faded coloration are conventionally used inside, but their forgiving surface suits all types of weather. The spirals in their patterning are similar to the fiddleheads of a soft shield fern (*Polystichum setiferum*) planted nearby.

OPPOSITE A glass fiber reinforced concrete chair surrounded by a colorful Japanese maple and a variety of textural plantings is designed to stay outside, but its sculptural shape would fit any contemporary interior.

Humor

When any room, inside or out, takes itself too seriously, it qualifies as stuffy. Humor plays a valid role in all spatial design and is prominent in a South London garden designed by Barbara Samitier, where guests walk outside and surprisingly find themselves in a perfectly appointed living room. By combining unexpected color and stylistic incompatibilities, she designed a lighthearted garden that is practical and attitudinal in equal measure. Her plays on scale, including the huge light fixture, towering walls of bamboo, and oversized pavers, exaggerate the humor even more. ⬎

HEAVEN SCENT

THE HARMONIOUS LAYOUT OF A WESTCHESTER COUNTY GARDEN designed by landscape architect Janice Parker reflects something the celebrated interior designer Andrée Putman once said: "For a house to be successful, the objects in it must communicate with one another, respond and balance one another." In this case, the objects outside the house—the pathways, allées, porches, guest cottages, decks, garages, vegetable garden, and even the chicken coop—are rapt in conversation. But when Parker first saw the property, it was cacophonous. Overgrown perennials and scrubby woodland plants created discordance, and because no one had established an intuitive way to navigate the land, there was no spatial harmony.

Once Parker moved and reshaped a driveway and protected some existing magnolia trees (her first priority), she transformed the back of the property into a series of intimate, functional living spaces in much the same way an interior designer might handle a capacious loft. She established terraces and a few choice spots for people to relax, chat, and eat. Then, using a less-is-more approach, she dialed back the hardscaping and plant materials and her limited material palette produced an overall sense of clarity.

The marriage of built and unbuilt areas in the garden now centers on views out to a harbor and marshlands. Parker built a low wall of squared boxwood with a stone border that wends its way toward the water. Perpendicular to the property's formal entry and oriented in the same direction, an allée of pleached linden trees flanks a bocce ball court. The area is underplanted with Siberian squill (*Scilla sibirica*), crocuses, and grape hyacinths, and when they bloom, the allée takes on a quiet sweetness.

Interior designer Anthony Baratta, known for his colorful twists on tradition, selected the outdoor furniture, and Parker keyed her plantings to his nostalgic colors and silhouettes. She brought in sumptuous, droopy hydrangeas in pinkish blues, and layered them with evergreens such as holly, arborvitae, and arching redbud trees. Bluestone risers are finished in a

dimensional rock-face style, with rustic, jagged surfaces. Unevenly sized stone pavers interspersed with grass form modified zig-zag patterns and seem to have been there forever. Bluestone slab steps are lined and retained by linear Cor-Ten steel planter boxes filled with deer-resistant herbs and flowers.

As with all of her gardens, Parker planted this one to be beautiful in all seasons, but its loveliness peaks in the spring. At that time, it glows light green with the foliage of beech trees and Eastern redbuds, as early flowering tobacco (*Nicotiana sylvestris*) and chartreuse sweet potato vines (*Ipomoea batatas* 'Margarita') start to deliver and fragrances of white clematis and lilacs fill the air.

A chicken coop Parker designed references the architecture of the 1922 house down to its cross-hatched doors and shingled roof, demonstrating how she devotes as much attention to minutiae as any interior designer. The vegetable garden, with its symmetrical layout of Cor-Ten steel boxes, is small and compact, but still produces an abundance of vegetables and herbs. ✧

Parker takes particular pride in the property's stonework, here surrounding a patio and dining area. The fronts of the bluestone steps project a shadowed dimensionality.

OPPOSITE Repeated beds of *Hydrangea macrophylla* 'Bailmer' are overtly pretty. Grass softens the edges of an asymmetrical stone path, making it feel even more organic.

Parker's pathways are as romantic as they are practical. Here, steps are flanked by dense bunches of Japanese forest grass that intentionally brush the ankles of passersby.

OPPOSITE A long sweep of yew hedge curves toward views of the bay.

Boxwood balls surround a chicken coop Parker designed for more than a dozen Rhode Island Red, Barred Rock, and Buff Orpington chickens.

OPPOSITE Cor-Ten steel planters contain annual plants and various vegetables as well as a mix of herbs, including lavender and thyme. A low stone retaining wall addressed surrounding grades, but was also a chance to introduce some rustic texture to a fence detailed by the architecture firm Shope Reno Wharton.

Alongside the bocce ball court, Cor-Ten steel troughs contain a mass of lilyturf.

OPPOSITE Rather than conventionally cut rectangular pavers, a path leading to the bocce ball court and an allée of pleached lindens has diagonally cut pavers with grass inserts.

Harmony

In music, the concept of harmony usually refers to a mellifluous arrangement, but in design, it often acknowledges the attraction between opposites, a technique Janice Parker utilized throughout this Westchester County garden. For example, stacked stone walls and planters constructed from Cor-Ten steel seem even more rugged and masculine alongside pastel-colored flowers and the feminine lines of retro furniture. To prove how contrary elements showcase each other's best attributes, the drama of her large, confident gestures, including sweeps of grasses and wide, meandering pathways, make the fine detailing in the hardscaping, borders, and metalwork more accessible. The harmonic blend of divergences is visually stimulating and feels distinctive because it defies any one, stylistic categorization. ↓

THE PLOT THICKENS

THE METICULOUSLY RESTORED 1730 STONE HOUSE owned by Frank Dunn and Hans Lupold in upstate New York retains many of its original features, including mouth-blown glass windows and wide-planked floors. The landscape surrounding the house has a similar charm as it slopes gracefully on its way to meet the edge of Esopus Creek and 1,200 acres of organic farmland. Surprisingly, the previous owners were somehow oblivious to the site's inherent beauty. They lassoed it with a tarmac driveway and sectioned it off with concrete slabs, railroad ties, and white plastic fencing. Over a three-year period, with guidance from landscape designer Marge Brower, Dunn and Lupold, who both have green thumbs, transformed the property. They trucked in yards of mushroom compost to balance the loamy soil after they contoured beds and laid foundational bluestone paths. They converted a disoriented vegetable patch into a stretch of lawn and replaced a row of large, mature pines with a white pine hedge. They added a porch to the back of the house and replaced a moldy 150-year-old barn.

The couple's principal challenge was to interconnect several of the garden's disjointed sections and replicate the same intuitive flow and intimacy they'd accomplished inside. Dunn, an architect who worked alongside the legendary modernist I. M. Pei for several years, grew up in stone houses and holds a strong affection for their period details. But outdoors, he satisfied his minimal leanings with the defined paths, crisp sets of steps, and well-edited, articulated beds. Most of the garden's walls are implied and demonstrate how well-constructed, dense vegetation can offer as much privacy as any fence.

Repetition is an important design tool for grounding and orienting space. Here, there is a calming effect from a controlled palette, where similar species reoccur from bed to bed and blooming periods are well sequenced. In late March, daffodils and crocuses emerge alongside forsythia, while an old magnolia tree and azaleas bloom. Then, ferns develop, along with hostas, peonies, lady's mantle, Japanese forest grass, phlox, roses, bleeding hearts, and Solomon's seal. Later, iris and hydrangea emerge. As the flowers of one plant die back, another's holds court—butterfly bush alternates with echinacea, mounds of white hydrangea give way to anemone, which ushers in the cooler weather. In the fall, several maples and golden beech trees shed their leaves, and once again open up views of the creek below to show the low autumn sun illuminating the water's glisten. By Thanksgiving, the trees are

OPPOSITE In their upstate New York garden, Frank Dunn and Hans Lupold used a variety of shrubs and trees with red, green, and variegated leaves alongside colorful perennials when they planted an animated border around their early-eighteenth-century stone house.

In the interior dining room, the table is surrounded by Dunn's great grandmother's chairs; outside, a contemporary wrought-iron dining set caters most of their casual summer meals.

OPPOSITE Repeated plantings of *Hydrangea paniculata* Quick Fire and a broad semicircle of Japanese forest grass help create a sense of movement in the beds at the back of the barn.

RIGHT An old magnolia tree shelters the commute to the barn, where lady's mantle, echinacea, several types of grasses, and 'Limelight' hydrangea border the path.

BELOW Along the pathway between the house and the red-sided barn, a bubbling fountain was a gift from Dunn's mother.

BOTTOM The Bill Merrill Sunset Terrace, a raised sitting area containing a table and four Adirondack chairs, memorializes a good friend and is thought of as the heart of the garden.

bare and leaves cover every horizontal surface, while red twig dogwood stems try to push their way through the debris.

The barn, a proportional replica of a reconstructed pool house, contains each of their home offices, so on their short, daily commute, Dunn and Lupold pass by beds of roses, Solomon's seal, red twig dogwood, hydrangeas, and smoke bushes. "I've grown to equate creativity with fragrant air, weed pulling, and butterflies dancing around a flower," says Lupold, who manages events at Mercedes-Benz. "Conference calls don't work so well, as the birds tend to sing along." ⬇

Alongside the swimming pool, a Lutyens-inspired bench is flanked by palms and potted annuals as well as bouquets of hostas.

OPPOSITE A sea of *Hosta* 'Sum and Substance' provides an appealing understory for a hammock.

Rhythm

Underlying visual patterns will encourage an interior or garden to flow or unfold organically. Frank Dunn and Hans Lupold's garden is easily navigated, thanks to an imposed rhythm, where repeated plants and varieties of the same species crop up in a natural manner, as if they had self-seeded. Every bed's border is purposefully defined and curvaceous to entice and motivate the eye onward. Recurring groupings of lady's mantle, hostas, and Japanese forest grass and an overall palette of purples, pinks, and lime greens define a familiar visual vocabulary. An interior designer may establish a similar subtextual rhythm in a room by letting a color or texture they extract from a central painting reappear on a textile, vase, window trim, or lampshade. ⤵

Linear rows of ostrich ferns (*Matteuccia struthiopteris*) and lady's mantle share a citrus palette.

OPPOSITE A weathered bench is permanently nestled into white pine and smoke bush branches.

MOOD

OPPOSITE As zinnias bloom throughout the summer, they symbolize endurance; as they attract butterflies and bees, they project optimism; and as one of the brightest, boldest of flowers, they elicit joy.

In Julie Hedrick's garden in Kingston, New York, nature is at its most optimistic when vibrant vines breathe new life into a weathered door.

THE INTRODUCTION OF COLOR— a coat of paint, a roll of wallpaper, a brightly upholstered couch, or a few throw pillows—is the quickest way to inject mood and emotion into a room. The way to inject the same sentiments into a garden is with a profusion of colorful, fragrant flowers. Eighteenth-century British poet Alexander Pope succinctly summed up the relationship between color and horticulture when he said, "all gardening is landscape painting," and, as it happens, many celebrated plant lovers, including Gertrude Jekyll, William Robinson, and Roberto Burle Marx, painted in their spare time. The reverse is also true: Claude Monet regarded his garden at Giverny as his studio; Georgia O'Keeffe treated morning glories and jimson weed as visual mantras; and whenever Frida Kahlo painted a zinnia or a fuchsia, she felt she was preventing it from dying.

Color preference is psychological, subjective, and chock-full of associations, but the way color affects and interacts with its environment is more logical. For example, a blue-gray room is thought to promote creativity, and flowers in similar hues situated close to a pond or pool neutralize some of the water's surface glare. Pink and blue have longstanding gender-specific associations with babies' bedrooms, but a sweep of pastel flowers is universally perceived as calming. Red and orange generate excitement, and when they're a prominent part of a room, they can draw people together and stimulate conversation. Outside, flowers in all shades of red, as well as bright orange, generate a similar energy, making them a sure antidote for a nondescript corner. Blacks, browns, and saturated dark colors in flowers or accessories tend to recede and visually push space back, which is why they are thought of as great disguisers.

Incorporating the four classical elements of fire, earth, water, and air into a design is mood enhancing whether the space is inside or out. Fire, the element of passion, fullness, and warmth, is associated with the colors of the sun. Indoor and outdoor fireplaces bring people together and, beyond providing warmth, encourage conviviality. The earth element represents transformation, nurturing, and fertility, and links to natural colors, corroded metals, terra-cotta, and wood. The water element, exemplified by a fountain, pond, or pool outside, and by ephemeral, blue and green color schemes and fluid shapes inside, is associated with harmony, feelings, and wisdom. Air is the element of intelligence, new beginnings, and creativity, and translates to greens and yellows and anything that mechanically moves or naturally interacts with a breeze, such as a weeping willow, a swing, tall grasses, a glider, and wind chimes. Inside, air is embodied by glass, diaphanous and billowing fabrics, tall ceilings, and open-plan rooms with few discernible boundaries.

When a design makes a point to acknowledge our five senses, the process of experiencing a garden deepens. Think of the aroma of herbs and flowers brushing against clothing; the sound of a footstep as it crunches into gravel or crinkles a pile of dried leaves; birdsong; or the wind rustling through a forest. The sense of taste isn't confined to a bountiful vegetable bed or an edible flower; consider the concentrated sweetness within a maple tree and the honeyed hum of a bee as it hovers over nasturtium or lavender. Wooly thyme, downy lamb's ears, pussy willow catkins, and the soft petals of a rose are all nature's equivalents to silks and velvets.

In the evening, as it takes on a new persona, a garden is at its moodiest and holds particular delights, especially when lacy shadows created by shafts of moonlight filter their way through a canopy of leaves. In the dark, a garden epitomizes mystery as night-blooming flowers, including jasmine, moonflower, and evening primrose, release their fragrance to lure, intoxicate, and seduce nocturnal pollinators. ⚘

OPPOSITE By expertly weaving the classical elements of fire, earth, air, and water into her balanced, symmetrically pleasing design of a garden attached to a weekend house, landscape architect Janice Parker addressed several aspects of Feng Shui.

BELOW, FROM LEFT TO RIGHT:

A tiny droplet of water conceivably elicited an emotional response from the Bengali poet Rabindranath Tagore, who once wrote, "Let your life lightly dance on the edges of time like dew on the tip of a leaf."

Daisies, some of the most innocent, purest of flowers, are surefire antidotes for cynicism.

The sight of a heavily laden apple bough, and the aroma, crispness, sweetness, and graspability of its fruit, satisfies all the senses.

BLUSH STROKES

IN A CASE OF LIFE IMITATING ART, when David Auch and Scott Flax were honeymooning in London a few years ago, they bought a fifty-year-old, abstract painting containing all the colors they had just used on the walls of their house in Santa Monica. In a case of life imitating nature, the wall colors—warm gold, fresh blue, anjou pear, olive, and blue-violet—were inspired by vines, stamens, buds, and stalks that thrive in the three small gardens located in the house's front, middle, and back aprons.

Wall paint and artwork are everyday topics of conversation for Flax. As an architectural colorist, he devises backgrounds for museum and gallery exhibitions, so his eye is as finely tuned as a perfumer's nose or a sommelier's taste buds. As evidenced by a black-and-white photograph of him pushing a wheelbarrow when he was a toddler, Flax's precocious relationship with gardening emerged at a young age. When he was eleven, and tending his father's vegetable patch in Levittown, New York, he planted zinnias in the shape of a huge color wheel so he could look out of his bedroom window and monitor the growth of the pie-shaped sections of flowers. Instead of zinnias, his current bedroom overlooks a healthy screen of silver dollar eucalyptus and Italian stone pine with shade-loving camellias at ground level.

On his property, the line separating the outdoor and indoor spaces is diffused enough for him to calculate all the garden areas as a part of the house's square footage. Some of the flowers, vines, and shrubs are so decoratively intrusive they could be wallpaper. They edge doorways and attach themselves to mullions between the window panes, keeping Flax ever aware of the subtleties in their growth. He encourages the plants to mingle with the structure of the house, for example he was so taken with the vivid colors in a honeysuckle vine, that he trained its new leaves to canopy above the kitchen windows. Exterior color also influenced many of the interior surfaces. After a friend, landscape designer Nancy Goslee Powers, planted a Mexican sycamore in the front yard as a gift, its bark prompted Flax to lay green-hued floor tiles in the house's main entry.

The front garden is the alfresco portion of the living room—a place to serve dinner, drinks, and dessert. Water bubbles out of a crevice in a large quarried rock that quenches the thirst of common and rare birds; Del Rio pea gravel covers the floor, with 2-foot-square concrete pavers laid on top to establish walkways, much like the way rugs cover portions of the oak floors inside.

OPPOSITE The textured bark of a Mexican sycamore tree inspired the floor tile in the house's exterior entry hall where Flax hung a glass pendant from the 1980s.

Like a good number of Flax's plant choices, the cascading bloom of lavender scallops (*Bryophyllum fedtschenkoi*) is both lyrical, hardy, and multifaceted.

OPPOSITE French doors in the dining room open onto a wall of bamboo and a cluster of potted flowers, including rosy-petaled dahlias, the inspiration for the room's wall color.

THIS PAGE When Flax selected the house's paint and fabric palette, he was influenced by the color nuances of the plant life growing close to each window or door, such as the clean yellow of a conical aeonium cluster, the pale green stripes of a tiger fig, and the pink tinge in a white magnolia bloom.

There's a textured interplay between the vibrant green conifers, the blue-violet coastal rosemary (*Westringia fruticosa*) flowers, the lavender, and the rosemary. Flax tends to zero in on attributes most of us would miss, and enthuses about the chromium-oxide green and powdery silver undersides of his favorite leaves. When a 100-foot-long fence covered with star jasmine is in its full glory, Flax gets emotional and refers to it as an absolute prize. But he's equally attuned to its less flamboyant phases; as it starts to retreat, he anticipates the honeysuckle canopy's headlining phase, when it's transformed into a white, yellow, and blue cascade. ⤵

In the living room, the furnishing material, carpet, artwork, and ceramics all relate to at least one aspect of the foliage or hardscaping in the garden.

In the front garden, water emerges and coats a boulder of black volcanic rock as magnolias mix with gold medallion trees (*Cassia leptophylla*) and *Podocarpus elongatus* 'Monmal' near a hedge of coastal rosemary. The Salterini wicker furniture is from the 1970s.

OPPOSITE The giant Burmese honey-suckle vine (*Lonicera hildebrandiana*) outside the kitchen window has been known to try and muscle its way inside.

Color

In design, when color palettes are likened to musical compositions, the comparison falls short, because although we are able to hear and appreciate a song or a piano concerto in its own right, color can never be appreciated in isolation. As it absorbs and reflects available light, it remains fluid, especially when it's influenced by neighboring materials. An interior design principle calls for 60 percent of a room, such as walls and ceilings, to be given over to a dominant, anchoring color; 30 percent should feature a secondary supporting color, perhaps in upholstery and draperies; and 10 percent should be devoted to an accent color, in pillows, accessories, and artwork. There's no such formula for outside. A rudimentary garden palette may rely on the color wheel's complementary and triad configurations, but for those of us who love uncomplicated solutions, one of the most poetic ways to paint a garden is to weave together plants, flowers, and foliage in multiple shades of a single color. ❧

HOUSE OF BLUES

OPPOSITE Charlie Ferrer, architect, was assisted by Richard Sammons of Fairfax & Sammons Architects when he designed a Palm Beach house and connected it to the garden, courtyard, and the greater landscape. On the patio, a pair of Alexander palms shade a pair of sky blue upholstered lounge chairs.

In an interior hallway, natural light enhances the blue and green hues in paintings by Mark Hagen and Friedel Dzubas.

THE HOUSE AND GARDEN COURTYARD Charlie Ferrer recently completed in Palm Beach, Florida, is so pleasantly cohesive, it's as if he was inspired by midcentury architect Eliel Saarinen, whose holistic approach always considered design in its next larger context—a chair in a room, a room in a house, and a house in its landscape. As a result, there's hardly any atmospheric separation between the interior of a white stucco house and its walled tropical garden: it is all one meditative piece.

Several aspects of Ferrer's scheme—he was responsible for the architecture, the interior décor, and the landscaping—contribute to everything feeling so well settled into its site. The lot is relatively compact, and he kept all the rooms proportionately small to subliminally reference the gracious time before zero-lot-line homes were so commonplace. His choice of weather-sensitive materials contributes another layer of nostalgia and makes the newly constructed project seem as if it were built decades ago. Limestone pavers, copper gutters, and bronze door hardware are already acquiring a patina and relinquishing their newness to Florida's salty air. His plan envisioned color as a connective tissue—the palette of oceanic blues in furniture upholstery repeats in a collection of contemporary art and on window shutters, so it's as if the elements of water, air, and sky have a reverberating presence.

Ferrer brought in mature foundational plantings, such as a date palm (*Phoenix canariensis*) and sea grapes (*Coccoloba uvifera*), which lent the site a timeless credibility as soon as they were planted. The foliage of plants installed around the house, and growing on it, including asparagus fern, creeping fig, jasmine, rosemary, philodendron, and waxy viburnum, is constantly trimmed back to encourage new growth and ensure that it all looks well tended.

In subtle and obvious ways, reflectivity is a leitmotif throughout Ferrer's design. It's a standard interior design trick to lean oversize, framed mirrors against walls to bring in light, open up cramped spaces, and play with perspectives, but Ferrer hung mirrors high, at least one to a room, to draw in vignettes of the garden and distribute glimpses of the interior. Sam Orlando Miller's multifaceted convex mirror in the living room captures a Richard Misrach photograph of a rippled ocean as well as the greenery in the courtyard. An oval mirror in the entry reflects the hedges outside. A starburst mirror in the loggia captures a reflecting pool.

The light-polished surface of the swimming pool and gushing fountains resemble glass in motion when bathed in sunlight. Even on the grayest day,

glimmers of sunlight dance on pearlescent mica in an antique mirror's decorative plaster. Throughout, all the floors are beige—whether wood, sisal, carpet, tile, or limestone—so there's a communicated sense memory of sand, so though the property is not literally on the shore, it has a beachfront mindset. ✓

Working with local landscape designer Mario Nievera, Ferrer trucked in mature trees, including blueberry (*Elaeocarpus decipiens*) and a pygmy date palm (*Phoenix roebelenii*), to take the edge off the garden's newness and foster a sense of heritage.

Ferrer planted greenery in close proximity to all the windows and French doors. In a guest bedroom, the fabric on a vintage sofa by Kirsten Holmquist, as well as the curtaining and wall paint, constitute a family of blues and perpetuate an atmospheric calm.

OPPOSITE When it flowers, a blueberry tree framed by a set of French doors extends the palette of the interior furnishings and art, including a blue velvet armchair by Ico Parisi, a sea glass lamp by Andrew Hughes, and a midcentury painting by Kenzo Okada.

Outside, a vine climbs the walls flanking beds of zoysia grass, where jasmine bushes and a pair of Christmas palms (*Adonidia merrillii*) line the way. In due course, climbing fig vine (*Ficus repens*) will camouflage the sides of the raised water feature.

A low hedge of ficus (*Ficus microcarpa* 'Green Island') divides the loggia from a bed of aquamarine water that reflects the structural columns as well as a broad expanse of sky.

Unity

Whenever a family of materials, patterns, forms, and colors is dispersed throughout an interior and its landscape, the stylistic ripple effect generates a sense of unity and calm. In a project Charlie Ferrer designed in Palm Beach, a shared aesthetic extends from the accessories all the way through to the architecture, so it's truly holistic. Ferrer began by developing a repertoire of materials and then overlapped and related them to every aspect of his scheme. His broad palette of blues is far removed from color matching, where the same shades are merely recycled and a sense of predictability sometimes sets in. Ferrer's way of highlighting relationships and drawing out similarities is a form of three-dimensional weaving, where all of the parts subliminally refer back to the whole. ↓

AWESOME ORE

JEFFREY BALE BELIEVES HE INHERITED HIS STONE OBSESSION from his paternal grandparents, who worked artistically with gemstones and rare minerals—not to mention his maternal grandparents, who built a large lava rock fireplace in their backyard and took him on trips to Petersen Rock Garden in central Oregon. Bale can still recall its water gardens and miniature structures encrusted with agate, jasper, lava, obsidian, petrified wood, and thunder eggs. Later, his interests took an international turn, when landscape architecture studies at the University of Oregon exposed him to the diversity of Islamic, Italian Mannerist, French, English, Indian, Japanese, and Chinese design. Consequently, his love of all things pebbled has prompted winter pilgrimages to geological sites the world over for nearly four decades.

Bale's garden in the Sabin neighborhood of northeast Portland is the consolidation of all the wondrous sights he has enjoyed on his travels. It's his interpretation of a maharaja's palace, where decorated surfaces are as intricate as handwoven fabric. In his exotic courtyard, inlaid stones and pebbles detail every wall, floor, pathway, bed, pond, and niche to produce a sybaritic sanctuary where he and his friends savor the sounds of birds and breathe in the aroma of tropical flowers. In the warm and dry weather months, he layers the courtyard floors with oriental rugs rather than furniture. A claw-foot tub plumbed with hot water doubles as a pillow-strewn daybed, draped with Laotian textiles and Indian saris.

When Bale found the property, it was a wasteland attached to a dilapidated drug den. After he carted away several dumpsters full of debris, he replaced an unfriendly perimeter chain-link fence with a grove of hardy banana trees. He added an Italian honey fig (*Ficus carica* 'Lattarula') and planted a screen of black bamboo. His elaborate stonework took seven years to complete—several thousand pieces went into the first retaining wall alone. Now niches are embellished with antique sandstone and artifacts from Thailand, Laos, Cambodia, India, Sri Lanka, and Peru, and protective symbols are in place to neutralize any residual energy from the property's former life. They reference spiritual practices from Native American mythology, to astrology, Vastu puranic design, and numerology. It took Bale six years to renovate two adjacent houses; their back windows face the garden and their brightly painted exterior siding recalls colorful Tibetan temples. Inside, the floors are dyed red, purple, and green, and a bathroom tiled with a panoramic mosaic of a fish-filled reef is the result of a two-year labor of love.

Most of the garden's greenery is contained within or embraced by stonework walls. When he selected plants, Bale considered leaf shape, size, texture, and fragrance rather than blooms, but bit by bit he has added flowers. Now vivid begonias overflow mosaic pots, ornamental rhubarb spills over onto a cotoneaster shrub, and star jasmine trails next to a variegated porcelain vine.

Every spring, an expressive emergence of native woodland plants sidles up against the smooth, matte stonework. Vivid ferns, trilliums, violets, hellebores, and Solomon's seal encircle a large kiwi and a century-old lilac, as boxwood loops around a Chinese ninebark (*Neillia affinis*) and several statuesque mahonia shrubs. Bale's neighbors are also beneficiaries of his extraordinary renovation. They particularly appreciate the climbing hydrangeas and pink-blooming dogwoods that envelop his house every summer. ✤

Persian carpets cover the garden's rock "patio" floor, and Bale transformed window frames and panels he brought back from Rajasthan, India, into niches. They showcase bronze reproductions of ancient Thai, Khmer, and Lao Buddhas as well as a carved marble statue of Shiva and Nandi the bull from Galta, Rajasthan.

A fig tree and the hardy leaves of a banana plant shade a tray table where Moroccan tea is about to be served.

BELOW Water spills quietly into a Rajasthani bowl next to a potted mukdenia (*Mukdenia rossii* 'Crimson Fans') and an elevated bed, where hellebore, variegated bamboo, and ornamental rhubarb appreciate the warmth radiating from the stone walls.

Details

It's easy to imagine guests removing their shoes when they enter Jeffrey Bale's visionary outdoor living room, because his use of textiles and carpets radiates such intimacy. His extraordinary focus is rare in any field of design. In his stone-inlaid garden, Bale selected each rock and pebble for its size, shape, and smoothness, and every symbol he depicts holds a backstory. The minutiae, the fine points of a color scheme or material palette, may seem subliminal, but they contribute enormously to the way a garden or an interior is experienced and enjoyed. They draw focus and create a sense of comfort, and then they politely recede so the overall scene can be appreciated in its entirety. ↓

A pebble path between two houses depicting a writhing rattle-snake is edged with Solomon's seal and native lady fern.

DEPTH OF FIELD

It's hard not to get bedazzled by the infinite array of green hues in Scott VanderHamm's woodland hosta garden. It's located in Poughkeepsie, New York, but even on cloudy days it has the lush exoticism of the tropics and as many leaf complexities as a jungle. In cool weather, it's an oxygenated microclimate where symphonies of color—gray-blues, neon limes, olive, jade, and emerald greens—pull together to form a rolling, textural quilt. Cupped, corrugated, variegated, and serrated leaves shaped like saucers, spirals, fans, platters, and plumes flow from vignettes, nooks, and alcoves.

VanderHamm is not a born gardener, and to prove the point, the first thing he did when he and his partner, Kren Shriver, bought their midcentury house was to sell its lawnmower. But after he was inspired, intrigued, and impressed by a friend's horticultural skills, he tackled his own acre of weeds and woods. He has now tended his family of hostas and forest plants for more than twenty years and, like his father, who evaluated each variety of vegetable he grew by weight at harvest, VanderHamm keeps meticulous records. At the end of each year, he files away all the care labels for any new acquisitions so he can refer back to them. His most up-to-date hosta spreadsheet caps his inventory at 250 different cultivars and 470 specimens. Why hostas? With upwards of 5,000 named cultivars, the enormous variety feeds his addiction for new specimens. Plus he enjoys their patterns of growth and the way their leaves and colors evolve throughout the growing season.

A square viewing deck extends from the back of the house, but otherwise the garden has no hard angles. Beds curve in circles and waves, weaving and overlapping, oblivious to beginnings and endings, to form an interconnected series of private spaces, hideaways, cubicles, and living landings. VanderHamm didn't start out with an overall plan and considers his plot to be an improvised art project, although he unwittingly plants with an awareness of what the ancient Chinese called the "principles of three depths." In this landscape painting convention, the foreground, middle ground, and background of each scene is configured according to a sequence of planes that add dimension. Consequently, his design never includes conventional walls, hedges, or fences—though a belt of 40-foot-high trees with trimmed canopies evenly spaced 12 feet apart supplies a superstructure that's both subliminal and appropriately imposing.

Other than the odd tree stump, the garden itself includes no seating—not even a hammock. The clear rhythm of VanderHamm's hierarchal planting style

OPPOSITE VanderHamm replicated the feel of a deep woodland by planting drifts of large-leafed *Hosta* 'Sum and Substance' amid clumps of segmented-leafed ferns and ligularia (*Ligularia japonica* and *L. przewalskii*).

In Scott VanderHamm's Poughkeepsie garden, gold and green variegated blades of Japanese forest grass flirt with plump leaves of *Hosta* 'Blue Mouse Ears'.

calls for ambulatory appreciation. The intoxicating, deep green immersion elicits a particular kind of calm solitude—a foundational fact known by interior designers, who treat green as a soothing neutral. Broad leaves droop onto a path as tall, multicolor grasses lie momentarily low, and a sharp breeze corrals the stems of three or four plants into a living bouquet.

VanderHamm's inner collector and designer are in a constant dialogue. The former is always on the lookout for new and novel introductions, and the latter envisions broad painterly sweeps of a single variety. At the end of the day, he takes a middle line, guided by each plant's personality and growth habits. Occasionally, he experiments by planting a hosta in sunlight, to watch its leaves work their magic as their color intensifies. Sometimes he falls in love with a cultivar name—the more evocative the better. Particular favorites include 'Tickle Me Pink', 'Church Mouse', 'Curly Fries', 'Pineapple Upsidedown Cake', 'Stained Glass', 'Sparkler', 'Rainforest Sunrise', or 'Maui Buttercups'—and the list goes on. ⌄

Trees supply textural structure for an underplanting of *Hosta* 'Love Pat', ghost ferns (*Athyrium* 'Ghost'), and a vivid dash of Japanese forest grass.

OPPOSITE Hierarchal plantings around trees include *Hosta sieboldiana* var. *elegans* and *H.* 'Autumn Frost', here enveloping the shaggy trunk of an Eastern red cedar.

THIS ROW, FROM LEFT TO RIGHT:

The platter-shaped leaves of *Ligularia dentata* 'Othello' take on a prominence when juxtaposed with the fronds of ostrich fern (*Matteuccia struthiopteris*) and a tree's scaly bark.

Plants with complementary leaf sizes include wiry-stemmed epimediums and 'Abiqua Drinking Gourd' hostas.

VanderHamm's hierarchal arrangements often include three or more plants. Here, epimediums provide a soft, green base for the fronds of an autumn fern (*Dryopteris erythrosora*) and the leaves of a variegated dogwood (*Cornus kousa* 'Summer Gold').

THIS ROW, FROM LEFT TO RIGHT:

Simulating a wall, chest-high fronds of cinnamon fern (*Osmunda cinnamomea*) cradle smaller plants such as *Pulmonaria* 'Moonshine'.

By planting seemingly disparate varieties in close proximity, VanderHamm creates sensual understories. Here he combined Japanese forest grass with *Hosta* 'Dream Weaver' and Japanese painted fern (*Athyrium niponicum* var. *dictum* 'Regal Red').

A boundary of craggy tree bark contrasts with the smooth variegated leaves of *Hosta* 'Gypsy Rose'.

An Eastern red cedar and two red maples provide vertical structure in one of several beds where dogwood and dwarf *Fothergilla gardenii* form groupings with low-mounding hostas, hellebores, and ferns.

Ligularia japonica produces buds shaped like miniature pumpkins.

Texture

Like a room painted in a monochrome—various tints and shades of any single color—Scott VanderHamm's woodland garden is encompassing and peaceful thanks to its network of intimate spaces and wide variety of textured, variegated leaves in a host of highly contrasting green hues. Whenever our tactile perceptions intensify, as they do here, a sense of calm prevails because our other senses become proportionately less active. Inside or out, whenever a group of textured surfaces is too similar, the scene will lack intrigue. But when coarse, smooth, or patterned surfaces coexist, there's an engaging visual weight when the rough and rugged set off the highly polished. This is why the tree barks in VanderHamm's garden provide not only structure but also a textural counterbalance to the silky hosta leaves. ⬦

Graphic leaf textures energize a jagged rock, including shaggy, dwarf woodland irises (*Iris cristata* 'Eco White Angel'), snaking leaves of an upright *Hosta* 'Praying Hands', and a shrubby Eastern white pine (*Pinus strobus* 'Nana').

An elevated deck on the back of the house overlooks
the entire garden, which is backed by a thick copse
of mature trees. A troughlike Cor-Ten steel container
planted with a 'Skylands' spruce blazes against a mix
of prostrate blue spruce and the purple blue leaves of
coral bells.

FURNITURE

As site-specific furniture, a recessed, semicircular seat transforms a brick wall's archway into a private nook.

WHEN ANY FAMILIAR OBJECT SITS IN A VAST LANDSCAPE, it orients us and helps establish a human scale, but the placement of a single chair does even more. In a wide, open space, it can also establish a room, and as we contemplate sitting down, we envision ourselves anchored firmly to the earth. Unlike a gate, a pergola, or another fixed structure, a chair instantly feels at home, and, whether it's placed on a slope or a stoop, it qualifies as a portable destination point. Small, well-edited groupings of furniture are inviting and invariably replicate the layout of an interior room, but large, crowded configurations of furniture are rarely hospitable. No matter how well arranged, they conjure up the temporary convenience of an airport lounge or a hotel lobby. They encourage guests to leave rather than stay.

A house feels more in touch with its surroundings when outdoor furnishings share the character and style of its décor. In the 1980s, Michael Taylor hammered the point home as one of the first decorators to bring outdoor furnishings inside, and in his interiors wicker chairs, slate tables, and fossilized stones coexisted with white slip–covered sofas and potted plants. His informal "California Look" hasn't really dated. It has been appropriated by the organic movement and still intermittently crops up in furnishing catalogues and shelter magazines.

Outdoor furniture is best constructed from hardy, nonwarping materials such as cedar and mahogany; resilient glass- and stone-topped tables are a good match for chairs woven from dried grasses, cane, and bamboo. When it's exposed to the elements, anything constructed from or detailed with metal, such as copper or bronze, oxidizes and garners a weathered, characterful patina. It "wears in" rather than "wears out." Period and vintage garden furniture tends to be large and solid and made from weighty materials like wrought iron and teak. In recent years, sleeker, scaled-down chaises, sofas, and benches with powder-coated steel frames have become popular because they fit into a range of garden styles, from minimal to traditional English. Along with garden gnomes, pink flamingos, and planters made out of old tires, design snobs like to turn their noses up at plastic outdoor furniture, but it's hard to dismiss its supermarket price, weight, and movability.

Inside, a wooden bench is often relegated to a hallway. It may replace a row of chairs alongside a dining table or double as a supplementary surface for a pile of books in a study. Outside, a bench comes into its own and invariably has pride of place. In and of itself it can demarcate a power spot, especially when it looks onto a distant mountain or a dramatic skyline. Whether it's refined, rustic, tastefully curved, or simply a spliced tree trunk supported on two thick logs, it's a solo statement piece. When a bench is enjoyed for its sculptural presence and rarely used, nature may intervene and cover it with moss or transform it into a trellis. Even so, it still subliminally tells us to slow down, relax, and stay a while. ✇

OPPOSITE In Stacy Sindlinger and Mark Rivett's Malibu, California, garden, a central fixture above the dining table provides supplemental light for moonlit meals.

BELOW, FROM LEFT TO RIGHT:

A weathered bench in Frank Dunn's upstate New York garden has matured into a quasi-trellis for a tight grouping of smoke bush, Japanese grass, and lady's mantle.

The spare, contemporary décor and long hallways inside a nineteenth-century brick-and-stone house inspired similar plantings and décor in the courtyards of a Yorkshire garden designed by Lee Bestall.

A metal chair, powder coated to match a bed of nearby irises, marks the best place to overlook a stream running through Ron Bricke's upstate New York garden.

MUSICAL CHAIRS

LANDSCAPE DESIGNER JOHN BROOKES ONCE ADVISED gardeners to use "half the number of plants and double the quantity." In the Arcadian garden Carl D'Aquino shares with his partner, antique dealer Bernd Goeckler, in New York's Hudson River Valley, the couple upped the quantity a hundredfold. There are exactly two foundational shrubs amplified to great effect on their ten-acre property—white hydrangea corridors and boxwood borders—and there's clarity in their bulk reiteration. It is as soothing as it would be in a large house if, say, a color or a textile were repeated at intervals. D'Aquino applied a similar principle to the property's perimeter, where more than 300 trees, including white birch, river birch, chestnut, maple, and copper beach, are grouped in fives and sixes to resemble natural copses. D'Aquino describes his theory as "density modulation." When the clusters alternate with open space, there's a subliminal rhythm.

The couple's mid-eighteenth-century red-brick house, filled with an elegant mix of Gustavian furnishings, sits at the top of a hill. In its current, graceful state, it's hard to believe that the house, like its garden, was a "train wreck" when they bought it. Now, since D'Aquino reconfigured and overhauled the landscape (and the house) with the help of his business partner, architect Francine Monaco, its gentle, lyrical slopes feel natural, though they are the result of clever terracing, lengthy retaining walls, and winding paths.

The dining porch is a few feet away from an ample chef's kitchen and a "pantry," which is how D'Aquino refers to his raised vegetable garden, and both serve as transitional rooms between the house and garden. Stylistically, the porch is a rustic version of the interior dining room, with two Viennese antler chandeliers and empty marble mirror frames hung on the walls.

A large area as deep as the south side of the house was raised to accommodate a formal parterre. Hydrangea shrubs infill hedges of boxwood pruned into geometric shapes punctuated by an occasional waist-high spiral topiary. Blue wicker chairs occupy the fallow spaces, their presence unexpected and hospitable. These empty chairs are less of an invitation to sit and more of what D'Aquino calls a "joyful conceit." At the head of the parterre, in the property's energetic center, stands a majestic sculpture of two inseparable lynxes, as if it's the garden's talisman.

Every year, cherry, peach, apple, and pear trees in the barn's orchard produce a bumper crop, but without netting, the birds are able to pilfer the lion's share. "They leave us less than half," says D'Aquino, "and that strikes us as equitable." ✧

OPPOSITE The layout of the dining porch at the side of Carl D'Aquino and Bernd Goeckler's house in the Hudson Valley is much less formal than the interior, but it too is guided by principles of symmetry. There are a pair of Viennese chandeliers circa 1900, two marble mirror frames, and a Lutyens bench flanked by metal Peyton barrels.

D'Aquino always places interesting objects at the end of each pathway to entice guests and to keep the garden animated.

PREVIOUS SPREAD The contemporary parterre is an orderly sea of clipped boxwood punctuated by crimson roses and lined by *Hydrangea paniculata* 'Limelight'. Wisteria is working its way across the house's brick facade.

LEFT The carved limestone sculpture (*The Loving Pair*, Holger Pedersen Wederkinch, circa 1921) depicts a pair of entwined lynxes and is the garden's energetic epicenter.

BELOW Similar to a costumier sewing a secret message into the seam of a gown, D'Aquino mounted a French cast-bronze stag head from the early 1800s high on the side of the house, where it is commonly overlooked.

OPPOSITE In a grove of white birch trees, an installation of pole-mounted bird-houses is surrounded by variously sized boxwood. A lichen-encrusted bench is more sculptural than functional.

CLOCKWISE FROM RIGHT:

In the orchard, apple tree boughs weigh heavier as the season progresses.

Several vintage tin watering cans, collected for their eccentric spouts, were sourced in local antique shops.

A mammoth seven-teenth-century trough outside the vegetable garden is carved from a single piece of limestone.

The back of the Julius Caesar bust can only be appreciated from inside the well house, which is primarily used as a potting shed.

ABOVE RIGHT A stern-looking, eighteenth-century Italian marble bust of Julius Caesar is stationed close to the property's original well house.

Flow

In his Hudson River Valley garden, Carl D'Aquino uses emphasis, focal points, and material repetition to create a pleasant flow. The eye is always egged on by a shape, a familiar shrub, a comfortable chair, a texture, or a repeated color. The circulation of any interior space can be designed in the same way. Clutter is often the main culprit when a space lacks visual or actual continuity. It's uncomfortable to linger in a space where the energy feels hampered. Outside, rhythm and flow can be curtailed by physical impediments—a path ending abruptly, a large rock obscuring a sight line, an overabundance of thresholds or transitions, or an excess of angular features. By avoiding these, D'Aquino's garden is animated, active, and participatory. It encourages you to move and it moves with you. ✛

ALL HANDS ON DECK

OPPOSITE On the front deck of Eduardo Rodriguez and Herman Vega's upstate New York garden, four high-backed armchairs placed symmetrically on a rectangular, striped rug create a private room.

Painted a citrus green, the house's main entry door ranks as the property's unique jolt of color.

BOTH HERMAN VEGA AND EDUARDO RODRIGUEZ grew up in Venezuela, with warm weather in their bones, so even though their upstate New York weekend house is hardly in a balmy climate, they furnished its garden as though it were.

Rodriguez, an interior designer, and Vega, creative director of *People en Español* magazine, wanted to plump up the personality of their tiny house, so they extended it into the landscape in a variety of ways. The path to the house progresses from the driveway with a hierarchy of materials—first gravel, then grass, then decking—and successfully keeps muddy footprints far away from this "shoes-off" household. Two tall black planters overflowing with grasses flank the lime-green front door and give the house "curb appeal," in Vega's words. The door opens directly into a great room with a cathedral ceiling, where one wall features a salon-style, floor-to-ceiling arrangement of paintings and photography. The house is set up to entertain, with lots of comfortable places to lounge, a chef's kitchen with a large dining table, and a well-stocked bar. But there is no entry hall or vestibule, so the couple set up an antechamber on the front deck. A rectangular rug establishes its boundaries, and four wing-back armchairs, one at each corner, surrounding a central table, keep the symmetrical grouping contained and clublike.

Outside, a dense ring of mature oaks and pines and low stone walls encircle the charcoal-colored house. The proportions of the front and back decks are calculated to exaggerate the width of the house, and the decking abuts its foundation, smoothing the transition from inside to outside. On the back deck, a healthy mix of angled and rounded shapes in the large-scale furniture seems appropriate to the openness of the site and tree heights, and the individual pieces suit Vega and Gonzalez, who are both tall. The orchestrated scale draws the eye in to create an energetic privacy and coolness on even the steamiest of days. The black, white, and gray color scheme of the exterior walls and furnishings feels almost neutral in this clearing in the woods. Graphic, geometric patterns crop up on area rugs, striped pillows, woven upholstery frames, and ceramic planters.

In the lower graveled sitting area, around a fire pit, four metal chairs define the room's wide perimeters. Each of these curved, industrial versions of traditional slat-backed chairs is draped with a soft sheepskin so they're hospitable in cold and hot weather. On the upper deck, the heights of a sectional sofa, coffee table, and ottoman are kept low, and streamlined to allow guests to socialize easily.

A planter filled with pruned boxwoods supplies greenery for the lower deck as well as a boundary for the upper level, as it separates the sitting and the dining area. Here and there, pots and vases filled with large, tropical plants and leaves echo the colors of the untamed, surrounding shrubbery. Every chair, side table, and sofa has a strong silhouette and feels resolved from all four sides—an important consideration when all the floating, spacious arrangements are visible from inside the house and feel as if they are a part of it. ⬇

Loftlike exterior "rooms" span the entire width of the house and all the furnishings repeat the black, white, and gray palette of the siding, roofing, and window trim.

FROM LEFT TO RIGHT:

Whenever black is used on the exterior furnishings, there's always a textural surface that reflects rather than absorbs light.

A suspended metal chair occupies a lookout position on the upper deck, allowing guests to survey a long view of the garden.

Rodriguez and Vega place objects, such as this metal ostrich, randomly on the edge of the property to draw the eye out to the surrounding woodlands.

FROM LEFT TO RIGHT:

A solid base and elliptical shape lets a practical cocktail table moonlight as a piece of sculpture.

The geometric shadows cast by metal-and-plastic Acapulco chairs increase their visual impact.

A waterproof rug provides a comfortable napping spot for Oliver, the family's French bulldog.

Pattern and Form

White, black, gray, silver, brown, and green act as neutrals when used outdoors. The black-and-white furniture scheme Herman Vega and Eduardo Rodriguez chose for their garden rooms is based on their house's interior palette and sets up an easy transition between the architecture and the surrounding woodlands. In each garden room, the furniture silhouettes are clean lined, with crisp upholstery and textures that enhance rather than distract from their shape. Patterns, stripes, geometric forms, and stark colors add dimension, with black functioning as a structural element, whether it's on the base of an ottoman, the cradle of a fire pit, or a suspended chair. ↓

SURREAL ESTATE

LIVING WALLS, PLANTED VERTICALLY AND WITHOUT SOIL, always feel revelatory. A dense organic curtain woven from ferns, mosses, shrubs, plants, and orchids is a wonderful way to defy logic. Today, thanks to the pioneering botanist Patrick Blanc, large-scale *murs végétals* are not unusual sights in Paris. What is unusual for Paris is to find a penthouse duplex in the eighth arrondissement with a courtyard, so when American architect Michael Herrman found one on the top floors of an eighteenth-century building, he was thrilled. Its dark, awkwardly shaped rooms and L-shaped layout felt too much like a catacomb, so Herrman made a dramatic decision to replace an interior courtyard wall and a section of flooring with glass panels. As a result, transparent walls on the sixth- and seventh-floors look onto a living wall of textured greenery, and the entire apartment is flooded with light.

As a theoretician, Herrman pushes his projects to reference the past, the spatially distant, and the illusory in some way. For this apartment, where he lives with his wife and daughter, he overlaid the renovation with a concept the architect Le Corbusier applied to a rooftop terrace in the 1930s. By consulting archival photographs, Herrman replicated some of the objects Le Corbusier had included in his terrace—a baroque fireplace, a gilded mirror, a birdcage on a stand—and staged them permanently in his own courtyard. His installation functions as an outdoor living area and simultaneously pays homage to a master of design. As the enclosed space is 15 feet tall and open to the sky, like any conventional garden it is sometimes immersed in morning fog, covered in snow, or pounded by hail.

Herrman grew up shuttling between New York, Paris, and Miami, so he's familiar with tropical greenery. Inspired by Blanc's living walls, he researched seventeenth- and eighteenth-century wallpaper patterns and based the layout of his own green tapestry on several swirling motifs.

For the most part, the foliage stays green year-round. In the fall, the courtyard's floor is layered with autumnal color as plants shed their leaves, making way for even more light to enter the courtyard and home. In the spring and summer, the wall turns purple with veronica, and flat leaves of ivy, hostas, and coral bells contrast with the spiky textures of blue fescue and a variety of other grasses. Sprigs of rosemary, lavender, and other fragrant plants attract pollinators and moths.

A 10-foot-tall mirror placed above the working fireplace blurs the inside-outside distinction, and as it reflects slivers of activity upstairs and

OPPOSITE Resting on the mantel of an operable marble fireplace in the courtyard of Michael Herrman's Parisian penthouse, a mirror reflects light and teases glimpses of an upper floor.

On the courtyard floor, sections of imitation grass match the scale of several weather-resistant hexagonal tiles salvaged from the site. The geometry continues with midcentury Bertoia chairs.

To continue the illusory effect established by the glass-paneled flooring, ivy trails on both sides of the window edges of the dining room and an upstairs sitting room.

OPPOSITE For the most part, Herrman set up a dialogue between the interior and exterior furnishings, and an interior pendant even mimics the courtyard floor's hexagonal tiles.

down, it adds another surreal layer. In the evening, the garden can be illuminated in two ways. The glow of an LED chandelier is best appreciated when the interior is dark, and lamps discreetly attached to the roof light the entire wall of vegetation, transforming it into the home's visual hearth. Small birds, including blue and yellow Eurasian blue tits, European goldfinches, yellow European serins, robins, song thrushes, and magpies are frequent visitors. They fly in from nearby boulevards, chirping at the novelty of discovering a slice of the countryside high up in the heart of the city. ⬇

The wall's plant palette includes switchgrass, rosemary, lavender, cushion bush, veronica, ivy, hosta, alumroot, blue fescue, and Japanese silver grass.

Surprise

Good design always incorporates unexpected elements, and in Michael Herrman's astonishing courtyard renovation, large and small surprises play pivotal roles. Predictability in design tends to dull the senses, whereas anything impromptu or improbable keeps us on our toes. Such as, at the end of a hall or pathway where a right-angled turn reveals a sudden change in a wall or plant color; a piece of sculpture tucked into a bookcase or bed of shrubs; a fragrant flower growing out of a compost pile; or a breathtaking wall of shrubbery on the top floor of an eighteenth-century Parisian building. Herrman could have installed a conventional furniture arrangement in his outdoor room, but instead he created an art installation that's both fixed and constantly evolving as it succumbs to the ever-changing weather. ↓

GREENERY SCENERY

At every turn, the eye is treated to a tactile feast, particularly wherever asparagus ferns, English ivy, and aeonium overlap.

TAKING HIS INSPIRATION from Russell Page's tailored viewing garden at the Frick Collection, in an early planning meeting with landscape designer Judy Kameon, architect Bill Georgis suggested dividing his La Jolla, California, garden into formal and informal rooms. "It was my New York attitude," he says. "I didn't necessarily want to see food being prepared while I was seated and about to eat." Kameon came up with a more relaxed approach, where the goings on in each interior room would simply spill outside, and her idea won out.

There was scant evidence of any garden when Georgis bought the midcentury house. The property was an indistinguishable tangle of invasive plants, with runaway ivy vines strangling eucalyptus and pine trees. But its setting, perched on a ledge parallel to a steep slope overlooking La Jolla Bay, with views of the Pacific Ocean and Mount Soledad, presented a wonderful counterpoint to Manhattan, where Georgis lives most of the year.

Inside and out, he undertook a massive renovation, reducing the house's four bedrooms to two, removing an addition, raising ceilings, and appending a cantilevering terrace to the house's front elevation. Now the building is slim, elegant, and one room deep. The dining room leads intuitively to an outdoor kitchen and an elevated grotto bordered by towering bamboo, papyrus, bird of paradise, split-leaf philodendron, and a massive banana tree. A library opens onto a sunny lounging area planted with a palm, rosemary, lavender, and gray-leafed coastal sagebrush. The master bedroom has a private fire pit and its own plot of succulents. The living room looks directly onto the pool, where guests are bathed in reflective sunlight and soothed by the sounds of trickling water.

By the time Kameon got involved in the project, Georgis had resolved the interior décor, with his characteristically sophisticated, witty, unique, and vivid style, and Kameon let it guide the palette and personality of everything she placed outside. Her plants emulate the warm whites, blacks, blues, bronzes, and golds of the art, accessories, and upholstery inside. Georgis's interesting tactile surface treatments—including silk velvet, cerused oak, seagrass, silver tea-leaf wall coverings, and a mirrored wall perforated with actual bullet holes—are a match for her tapestried plant walls featuring masses of tendrils, vines, craggy trunks, and enormous leaves. Georgis's furniture plans are layered and exuberant; Kameon's vegetation is lush and pronounced. She added fully grown olive trees to match the boldness and maturity of his work. "There's a level of engagement when you're pressed up against plants," says Kameon, a premise Georgis clearly applies to all his furnishings.

San Diego's subtle seasons enable Georgis to swim in his backyard pool and cook outside throughout the year. Fire pits warm cooler evenings, and in all seasons the garden is illuminated by the pool's surreal glimmer. Kameon's plant choices, including agaves, stonecrop, Japanese maple, aloe, and dark purple New Zealand flax have a showy longevity. Fragrances from leaves of climbing rosemary, eucalyptus, and sage surround the occasional flower. "I didn't want any at all, but Judy snuck them in," says Georgis. "And it's an extraordinary moment in the spring and summer when the plumeria blooms and the air is full of frangipani. Totally magical." ⌄

OPPOSITE Pink-flowering ice plants trail from the pool walls in front of cordylines and palms.

A Danish Egyptian–revival chaise and a Bavarian deer-legged stool are upholstered in sleek fabrics that toy with the dense texture of the foliage outside.

Succulents soften the tread and riser angles of a set of travertine stairs on the approach to a conversation area that's notched into the hillside and studded with a large-leafed bromeliad (*Vriesea imperialis*) and a 'Hercules' aloe.

OPPOSITE Overhead heating takes the edge off cool evenings when guests dine outside at a Norman Foster table. A chocolate vine (*Akebia quinata*) covering the pergola provides dappled shade on sunny days.

OPPOSITE The dense understory around a seating area mixes agaves, a bushy westringia, and a flaming cabbage tree.

BELOW Opposite leaves attract as a needlelike jelly palm meets a curvaceous kalanchoe.

ABOVE The dimension in Kameon's planting creates light play between the curling leaves of a jelly palm (*Butia capitata*) and its fruits.

ABOVE RIGHT Along the hillside at the front of the house, tiny leaflets of an olive tree are accentuated by tactile plantings of juniper and deep red New Zealand flax (*Phormium* 'Black Adder'), along with low-growing grasses and groundcovers.

Integration

There are many ways to integrate a house with its surrounding landscape. Bill Georgis and Judy Kameon's collaboration achieves it spatially and stylistically, so there's a layered symbiosis between the architecture, interior design, plant palette, the landscaping, and the exterior furnishings. This holistic treatment makes the garden flow into the interior particularly because Kameon translated the DNA of Georgis's aesthetic into horticultural terms. Most importantly, the indoor and outdoor spaces are atmospherically similar, which wouldn't have been the case if Georgis had followed through on his idea to divide the exterior into formal and informal sections. ↓

TIME

OPPOSITE Neil Sutcliffe of Creative Roots in Nottingham, England, satisfied his client's need for visual peace and tranquility by designing a Zen rock garden based on time-tested principles, including asymmetry and concealment.

Given the right amount of shade, within a few seasons a newly planted sweep of ferns turns into a unified, textural mass.

WHEN WE WALK INTO A HOUSE, its surfaces, smells, and colors, along with the style and provenance of its furnishings and artwork, speak to its age. They convey a sense of its period and the length of time it has taken to evolve. Making that same kind of evaluation in the garden is trickier but more rewarding, because nature links us to the past, the present, and the future. We know some things for sure: A radish seed needs about four weeks of measured growth before it becomes edible. Some hibiscus flowers open in the morning and wilt by midafternoon. Olive trees can live and continue to bear fruit for hundreds of years. It's deceptive to judge a garden's maturity by its overall fullness or to think of a room's many layers as a mirror of its owner's varied life experience, because skilled designers know how to instill a sense of age and character into their brand new creations.

Chintz fabric and flocked wallpaper evoke a sense of nostalgia in a room, just as old-fashioned flowers make a garden appear to have existed for generations. The rose, for instance, is equally conversant with contemporary or traditional gardens in every part of the world. If you examine a fabric's seams or a table's joinery, you can likely decipher its age, but this is impossible to do with a perennial. The Rose of Hildesheim in Germany, for example, was planted in the early ninth century, and every year it still blooms anew with its heady fragrance intact. The unabashed sweetness of roses, along with foxgloves, hollyhocks, primroses, peonies, and bellflowers, conjures up images of the past, just as trellises of sweet peas, vines of morning glory, pots of heliotrope, and fences lined with poppies and larkspur remind us of times gone by. And yet, each easily adapts to contemporary surroundings.

It would be sacrilegious not to preserve a living room's antiques, but we willingly let a vintage bistro chair or an urn rust in a newly established garden, because patina implies experience and an indeterminate age. When we place a few treasured objects in the landscape and let nature take its toll, we transcend the immediate time and place and end up with a meaningful metaphor for time's passage, progression, and transience.

A wall of Venetian plaster or a faux finished surface immediately gives a room a historical context, just as rough-hewn wood planks or stone pavers suggest well-trodden floors outside. These quick transformations instill age, but nature's authentic time-honored pacing and signs of maturity will not be rushed. Ivy takes years to trail across the outside of a house, and wisteria takes just as long to smother an arbor. When we encounter evidence of time having passed in nature, it's so much more compelling and more satisfying than anything man could ever make.

Statistically, people who swear by the superior taste of heirloom vegetables are likely to cherish objects they've inherited from previous generations. Certain people who collect books, china, and artwork see themselves as custodians rather than owners, as preservationists who are invested in the past as well as the future. Most gardeners share that sensibility and consider the act of planting a seed to be a long-term investment. When a gardener adapts to a plant's mindset and intuits its growth trajectory, he or she is synchronized with the universe's death/renewal cycle, and linked to eternity. ✤

OPPOSITE In the forecourt of Carl D'Aquino's upstate New York garden, wood-and-metal folding chairs are left to weather so they become more patinated and character-full.

BELOW, FROM LEFT TO RIGHT:

When hellebores begin to grow in late winter, often poking their way through a thick layer of snow, it's as if they are defying time's natural order.

The curls, crotches, and burls in a slab of walnut—here transformed into a table in Jon Gilman and Brad Learmonth's garden in the Hamptons—are all reminders of nature's maturation process and its resilience to time.

When deteriorating walls in a living room or on a porch bear the traces of past generations, they put the present into a broader context.

KARMIC CALM

AS A CHILD WHO DOUSED HER MOTHER'S ROSE BUSHES with cans of 7-Up to quench their thirst, Laura Hull was naturally benevolent to plants. She went on to cultivate window boxes and tend communal vegetable plots, but her current garden is truly allowing her horticultural instincts to flourish. When Hull, a photographer, and her husband, architect Mark Stankard, bought their half-acre property in Altadena, California, it was difficult to detect what, if anything, was salvageable. Ten-foot-high bamboo stalks grew rampant around decaying fruit trees. Tenacious, self-seeding geraniums peppered sweeps of waist-high grass. When the couple eventually found an original plan of their lot, prepared in 1957 by landscape architect Courtland Paul, who was known for his indigenous designs—as well as his wardrobe of saddle shoes and bowties—lots of things started to make sense. A dilapidated structure turned out to be a modernist fountain. They shelved a plan to stucco a wall made of concrete blocks once they realized its rawness was intentional, and they adopted Paul's terminology for their portico, which they now call a lanai.

Based on a new master plan created by landscape designer Wynne Wilson, whose nearby garden had inspired them for years, the couple rejuvenated their plot with drought-tolerant and predominantly native plants similar to those that grow voluntarily in the nearby foothills of the San Gabriel Mountains. In all likelihood, the fruit-eating bears, coyotes, skunks, possums, raccoons, bobcats, birds, and other regular visitors from the animal kingdom see Hull's pair of raised vegetable beds as an "all you can eat" salad bar. But Hull doesn't mind sharing her bumper crops of artichokes, peppers, onions, lettuces, arugula, tomatoes, basil, strawberries, chard, and kale. From an elevated deck outside the living room, the garden below appears orderly yet wild. Hedges of pineapple guava (*Feijoa sellowiana*) planted next to a new retaining wall surround a dwarf blood orange tree and fruit-filled olive trees. A scattering of flowers and berries in hues of purple-blue features penstemon, blueberries, native irises, ceanothus, and sage.

The young garden is still trying to establish itself, but it has its multigenerational aspects. More elderly than its decades-old skeletal structure is a group of rare bonsais Hull inherited from the late ceramicist Paul Soldner that were likely forged from century-old specimens. Hull is also espaliering some mission figs and avocados she transplanted from a previous house, and her orchids go back even further.

Hull and Stankard managed to balance the atmosphere between the house and garden so the transition is continuously calming and serene. The pale and muted color schemes are similar in both environments, and the interior floor of whitewashed panels of wood closely matches the deck flooring and the gravel in the garden. Stankard wanted a conventional lawn, but Hull persuaded him to agree to sedge grasses—her environmentally sound riff on a midwestern lawn—and they were both pleased to retire their mower. ⬇

Hull and Stankard considered installing a living roof on the lanai but instead opted for maintenance-free gravel, the same kind they used on the pathways. Rather than a standard lawn, the couple chose low-maintenance, drought-tolerant sand dune sedge (Carex pansa).

In the private, enclosed courtyard outside the master bedroom, a red butterfly chair provides an unexpected dash of color. A bubbling water feature built around a Buddha head acts as a lullaby and extends the home's peaceful atmosphere.

The interior ceiling cantilevers outside over a deck and, with the help of floor-to-ceiling windows, extends the perceived size of the living room. Inside and out, the furniture is either neutral or white.

OPPOSITE Six inherited bonsai trees mounted high up on terra-cotta columns on one side of the lanai are protected from animals and partially sheltered from the elements.

A restrained palette of plants as well as hardscaping materials—gravel on pathways and roofs, concrete fountain, retaining walls, birdbath, and planters—contributes to the garden's unified sense of calm.

A contained, floor-to-ceiling wall of books leaves the living room clutter free and full of air. Low furniture heights as well as walls of windows leave panoramic views of the garden open and unobstructed.

Neutrality

When considering colors, interior designers have endless possibilities, but the color green is a given baseline outside, where it ranks as a neutral. Some gardeners evaluate a flower according to the color of its bloom, but Laura Hull considers the entire plant. As a result, her garden features lots of blue-gray and silver flower heads, stalks, and foliage. Her garden beds feel like textural wings of her house's predominantly white interior. The grays and whites start to recede at dusk, and then the garden reads as distinctively blue. ↓

SUN WORSHIP

REALTORS IN LAGUNA BEACH, CALIFORNIA, were undoubtedly shocked when Greg Salmeri reduced the size of his house from 10,000 to 3,900 square feet. Owned by his family since the 1950s, it began to feel unmanageably large after Salmeri's mother died, and although it held a trove of memories, he felt more allegiance to its surrounding land, where he played as a child. As an adult, he witnessed the garden's style evolve according to his mother's whims—from tropical to overfed and bloomy. In its current Mediterranean iteration, it commemorates his trips to Provence and Tuscany, so his attachment to this particular piece of earth continues to strengthen.

Salmeri has lots of neighbors close by, but thanks to the leveled terrain and the intricacies of his plantings, they fade from awareness. The delicate colors and textures of the beds planted throughout the property draw the eye inward and then out toward the dramatic expanse of the Pacific Ocean. The open layout is reminiscent of a loft space, where intimate areas are dedicated to a particular purpose. The alfresco dining room is the most structured part of the property, protected under a covered portico dripping with wisteria vines. The bocce ball court, according to Salmeri, is more fun than a swimming pool and requires zero maintenance. A pillowed chaise surrounded by greenery is turned in the direction of Catalina Island. Clusters of rosemary, bay laurel, and geranium anchor a group of chairs and simultaneously proffer a mini aromatherapy session.

The path to Salmeri's profession, as a designer and co-owner of Rolling Greens Nursery, was paved by his artist-horticulturist mother. Growing up in Arizona and frustrated by her inability to grow her favorite flowers there, she devised a way to ice lilacs until they were cold enough to form blooms. She smeared sugar and honey around the tops of peonies to encourage ants to eat their protective layer and watched them miraculously open. In a case of the apple falling close to the tree, Salmeri's "wing-it" approach to gardening favors intuitive happenstance over strategic planning, and he constantly flirts, and invariably succeeds, with plants that aren't conventionally designated for California's growing zones.

Unlike many of the modernist residences in the neighborhood, Salmeri's house and garden are not literally and visually linked through walls of windows and sliding glass doors, but the timeworn antiques he lives with share a sensibility with his mature gardens. Both have an inviting air of informality. After years of experience, Salmeri knows how to layer age onto the new projects

OPPOSITE In an elevated part of the garden, a teak opium bed is screened by butterfly bush, geranium, and Italian cypress. The sun gradually eroded the pattern of several tiles Salmeri randomly recessed in the gravel.

Sedum 'Autumn Joy' is planted prolifically throughout the garden, like a leitmotif.

In the front pathway leading to Greg Salmeri's Mediterranean garden in Laguna Beach, California, a potted dragon tree (*Dracaena draco*) has a collar of scented geranium. Climbing roses decorate the corner of the house outside the sitting room window.

A roof-high dragon tree, potted in an olive jar, wears an apron of aeonium as it stands adjacent to the house's main entrance.

OPPOSITE Multicolored, blooming vines embellish an ornate, wrought-iron balustrade on a small balcony off the master bedroom.

he creates for his clients. He always prefers to source vintage furniture, statues, and urns with existing patinas and perhaps even a crack or two. He often plants dense groundcover around the legs of a chair, sofa, or bench, so it appears to be rooted to its spot. He top-dresses with decomposed granite and gravel and prefers old stones and imperfect pavers. He welcomes the prospect of the sun bleaching the vibrancy from fabrics or patterned ceramic tile.

He established the garden with white- and purple-flowering ornamentals, but now its palette includes every color imaginable. He struggles with pink, and would never pair it with yellow; he avoids plants with large leaves that tend to hog the limelight. "I'm definitely biased toward anything drought-intolerant," he says, "but watering the yard is my main form of therapy, and as I'm in constant need of that, nothing here ever goes dry." ⬇

Vintage French chairs grounded by a patch of euphorbia and stonecrop occupy a spot where the path widens.

OPPOSITE Above the 12-foot-long reclaimed-wood table, a wisteria vine climbs an arbor Salmeri fashioned from vintage French drain pipes. He wired the chandelier to hang upside-down, so it doesn't catch the rain.

A rusted gate leads to the lower garden. Salmeri glued the lions to pillars where rosemary, jade, and agave thrive.

A Chinese wine jar Salmeri inherited from his mother is concealed within a thicket of lobelia, blueweed, and olive tree branches.

A densely planted slope in the front garden features *Agave* 'Americana' and *A.* 'Attenuata' punctuated with bushes of rosemary, blueweed, and coastal westringia.

Coordination

Although Greg Salmeri's house and garden aren't literal extensions of each other, they share a like-mindedness. Needless to say, the interior's textiles and furniture are more precious than those used outside, but, stylistically, they are all simpatico. For example, all the holes and loose yarn in the antique rugs in his living room are comparable to the garden's well-trodden gravel paths and crumbling stonework. In his mind, his olive tree and his living room's antique leather couch are buddies. He draws a parallel between the threadbare nap of vintage upholstery and the garden's spent flowers. Salmeri reckons he could easily move all of his outdoor pieces inside and live with them. ⬦

ROMANCING THE STONE

OPPOSITE An unglazed clay vessel by ceramicist Sylvia Benitez has a permanent spot in front of a galvanized shed Sarah Draney designed with Eric Freeman.

House shapes figure prominently into the sculptures Draney creates using materials from her upstate New York garden. A bird feeder, filled with hulled sunflower seeds, perches between a thriving butterfly bush and some leafy Japanese basil.

HAILING FROM A FAMILY OF HORTICULTURALISTS, Sarah Draney played in gardens throughout her childhood and can't recall a time when she wasn't gripped by nature's impermanence. Twenty-five years ago, when she started gardening on her own property in upstate New York, she had relatively few ambitions. She envisioned a humble rockery attached to the modest house she and her husband had built on eight woodland acres, with creeping thyme and other aromatic herbs spilling out of crevices. She would tend and water it when she took breaks from painting and sculpting in her second-floor studio.

But her connection to the landscape turned out to be more profound and deep rooted than she'd anticipated, and the more her rockery inspired her, the larger it grew. In the beginning, she expanded it with boulders and slabs of flat stone sourced from local quarries. She laid gravel pathways and staged them with found objects, including rusted cogs, dilapidated bedposts, cracked pipes, and other random paraphernalia she found in local junk shops. She turned her house's wraparound porch into an impromptu gallery by arranging textured planks, weather-beaten chair frames, and assemblages of twigs, rusted objects, ceramics, and ancient farm implements.

One day, as she leaned one of her ceramic trays against a piece of corroded metal and their surfaces were barely distinguishable, she had an epiphany. From then on, as she constructed ladders from dried flower stalks and engineered teepee-shaped sculptures from fallen cedar branches, she realized that the line dividing her garden and her art studio had evaporated. Once she acknowledged nature as her muse and mentor, her work truly matured.

In her studio-cum-garden, her own creations and a multitude of weather-worn found objects define one kind of beauty, while a variety of perennials, grasses, shrubs, and roses define another. When Draney introduces a new plant, she coddles it for a season or two before leaving it to its own devices; consequently, all of her plant specimens are hardy and drought-tolerant. Despite her tough love, most plants thrive here, and, while her neighbors treat lavender as an annual, in her microclimate, it "lives over," as she puts it. With so many stones and pea gravel doubling as mulch, the garden has perfect drainage as well as a temperate environment for Mediterranean plants.

While general attitudes toward weeds have altered since Draney first started her garden—these days, the edible variety are a staple in pricy farm-to-table restaurants—her vision still holds as unique. One of her inspirations was Derek Jarman, the late filmmaker whose Prospect Cottage garden on the

English coastal town of Dungeness punctuates greenery and shingle paths with twists of driftwood and flint markers. Another like-minded embracer of decay is Dutch nurseryman Piet Oudolf, who once defined his favorite garden as an abandoned steel factory, where self-seeding plants had taken it upon themselves to emerge from cracked walls. The late gardener Christopher Lloyd had a great affection for self-sowers. He often referred to them as allies who needed to be well controlled. ⬇

OPPOSITE, FROM LEFT:

Volunteer plants grow around a strip of wood as if it's a stalk.

Shiso thrives in Draney's garden, where it appreciates the warmth provided by lichen-covered stone borders.

THIS ROW, FROM LEFT:

Draney creates assemblages in her garden studio, where natural features and her organic artwork are like peas in a pod. Here, she matched a self-seeded euphorbia with a grouping of stones and a rusted screen.

Broken rounds of aggregate are juxtaposed against the gray-green, heathery fronds of artemisia.

A rusted cog, a rose-colored brick, and some iron lattice offer weathered beauty.

A fragment of rusted screening leans on lichen-dotted stones.

A stalk of dried mullein stands out against a dense planting of zebra grass.

THIS ROW, FROM LEFT:

Red-leafed shiso (*Perilla frutescens*) grows alongside a weathered shed wall.

Draney surrounded one of her porcelain containers with air moss she gathered around her property.

Gangly stalks of mullein remain in Draney's garden throughout the winter to provide textural interest as well as food for birds.

Draney dries flower stalks, some up to 15 feet tall, to use in ladder and grid sculptures.

Personalization

When self-expression is the basic philosophy behind a design, the result feels refreshingly genuine. Sarah Draney's unique vision for her alfresco studio illustrates her individualistic approach to her life and art, where she celebrates the weeds in her garden as much as her cultivated flowers and embraces nature's cycles of growth and deterioration in every form. *Wabi-sabi*, a Japanese aesthetic centered on the appreciation of transience and imperfection, is often used by designers to balance the bristling newness of a recently completed project. Beauty can be found in all things imperfect—a threadbare rug, a tarnished silver vase, faded fabric, or a porcelain vase with a hairline crack. Draney's garden is a living example of this aesthetic. ↓

Like decaying driftwood, two collapsing Adirondack chairs settle into the forest at the property's edge. Along with a small fire pit, the area is invigorated by lively clumps of vivid Japanese forest grass.

OPPOSITE On one of the house's porch galleries, above a grouping of weathered boulders and a marble finial, an assemblage includes an antique wicker chair, a barrel hoop, a gnarled tree root, and a metal box used as a pedestal for an assortment of Draney's ceramic pieces.

GRAND ALLUSION

as a "gardener/furniture mover," but her reputation as one of England's top interior designers has been established since the 1980s, when she opened Blake's, London's first luxury boutique hotel, in South Kensington. There she unleashed her theatrical panache for dressing interiors, and these days, as the owner of an internationally esteemed design firm, her style is inimitable whether she's furnishing a big city pad or a hotel suite in a rain forest.

In the mid-1980s, she and her husband bought Cole Park, a moated, medieval manor in Wiltshire, and its landscape illustrates how well her skills extend to gardening. Over the centuries, the property had functioned as a monastery, a gigantic orchard, and a royal stud farm. Its sixteenth century manor house had been extensively and progressively altered. Depending on the viewing angle, its stone-and-brick facade qualified as either Tudor, Queen Anne, or Georgian, so Hempel neutralized it by creating a living annex, a rectilinear allée of mature white chestnut trees. Its scale is on a par with the house and the peacefulness in its order, geometry, and line deflects from the house's architectural hodgepodge.

This grand, processional gesture is contrasted with Hempel's more attentive plantings closer to the house, where whimsical pots filled with mushroom-shaped boxwoods are huddled together on plots of raked gravel. Arbored wisteria flanks flawless pathways, as the smell of gardenias, jasmine, and honeysuckle punctuates the air. Bucolic swans glide regally on the moat, and Suffolk Cross sheep graze in stone-fenced fields. All the house's exterior doors open onto a precisely formed pathway or a circle of grass or something tapered and tailored, but never an herbaceous border, because they remind Hempel of "little old ladies with their bottoms in the air."

In all likelihood, Cole Park's grounds were never as elaborate as they've become since Hempel took charge. At some point early on they may have been compartmentalized—possibly with turf benches enclosing beds of medicinal herbs. Her exterior rooms share the visual language of her interiors. Outside, there's always a sense of human scale, of a room within a room; inside, each of her signature bedrooms contains a curtained four-poster bed, so guests can sequester themselves in a room within their room, if they so wish. She treats stone pathways and hallway carpets with the same flair, and all invariably end with a visual delight. Outside, she offsets an unappealing view with a screen of trees or hedges; inside, she does the same with a

OPPOSITE In Cole Park, Anoushka Hempel's garden outside of London, a snow-covered row of lindens looks just as majestic in midwinter as it does in the height of summer.

Uniformity is key in the pleached linden allée, where Hempel's gardeners use templates to keep the trees pruned to an exact shape and size. The canopies of horse chestnut trees are likewise all trimmed to a consistent height.

In one of Cole Park's many dining areas, a teak table and benches are positioned to take in a view of the moat. At night, glass lanterns illuminate mushroom-shaped boxwood topiaries with candlelight.

Architectural finials that once decorated a dome, cupola, spire, or gable are now surrounded by pots of carefully pruned boxwood and lime trees. The striped pots recall the age-old tradition of painting young tree trunks white to prevent their bark from splitting.

BELOW Hempel creates a rhythmic pattern with flat and spherically shaped boxwood. Gravel covers paths and crops up in swirls and geometric patterns on areas of lawn.

lacquered screen or a curtain. Outside, expansive dining areas conceal intimate spots where guests can sit and reflect; inside, grand labyrinthine rooms contain secretive nooks and crannies.

Hempel's garden maintains its structural beauty throughout the winter. When trees are stripped of their leafy clothing, and their skeletons reveal their hardiness as well as their fragility, they become poetically vulnerable versions of themselves. In her uniquely witty way, Hempel has pithy advice for any winter gardener: "When it snows, don't just sit and stare at it," she says. "Go outside and create your own nonsense. Get a shovel and make huge white swirls around the base of a tree. And always remember to cover your tracks!" ⬇

OPPOSITE Potted hostas and colorful ceramic basins line a stone path leading to a dining area where obelisks provide vertical structure and contribute to one of Hempel's signature symmetrical arrangements.

OPPOSITE Boxwood hedges are trimmed precisely, and a spirit level ensures that all their lines are straight and perfectly angled.

Like a dusting of powdered sugar, the first substantial fall of snow transforms an angular boxwood hedge into visual confection.

A long Belgian bluestone-and-slate table sits on a carpet of black gravel. Used mainly for summer parties, it's screened by rectangle-pruned hornbeam hedges and yellow catalpa pollards.

Layering

As well as intimate and aesthetically pleasing, Anouska Hempel's characteristic layering is both structural and functional in interior and exterior designs. A hallway screen conceals the bottom of a staircase and creates an element of intrigue; outside, a battalion of potted, manicured shrubs of various heights placed around a table creates a private boîte. The adaptability and movability of Hempel's design layers appear spontaneous, even though the arrangements have been meticulously planned. An integral part of any garden's makeup, layering creates density and depth when it involves a variety of low to high planes, from hardscapes to canopies, and from borders to trellis tops. Fundamentally, layering plants requires an understanding of each plant's growth pattern and its habit of developing and spreading horizontally or vertically. ⌄

HOME SWEET HOME

TWENTY-FIVE YEARS AGO, when David Urso first spotted the house he now shares with his partner, Dennis Nutley, silhouetted on the crest of a hill flanked by catalpa trees, it reminded him of a jewelry box. Built in 1929, it presides over a charming, parklike enclave in upstate New York, which likely hasn't changed much since sibling Norwegian hoopers first settled there in the late 1800s. As soon as the couple took ownership, they renovated the house, faithfully matching any new millwork to the living room's original fir fireplace. "Inside and out," says Nutley, "to us, it feels like old times."

The house's extroverted front facade, with its steeply pitched portico, commands a panoramic view of the Catskill Mountains, but the three-acre parcel behind the house is slim and secluded. The land was and still is edged by a glade of mature oaks, maples, and pines, but back then it was overgrown with milkweed, white pine, and berries and served as a pit stop for grazing deer and wild turkeys. Today, the main garden is laid out like a house, with rooms on either side of a central corridor. Each space is interconnected, yet self-contained, comfortable, and functional.

Because of the prevalence of shale, the garden's ever-evolving design is determined by the topography and depth of soil, as well as three microclimates. In a gravel-covered courtyard, crisp, interconnected sitting and dining rooms surround a natural gully pond where several generations of koi have grown fat. Up an incline, a privet archway leads to an open field and a hybrid cutting and vegetable garden, where raised beds provide multitudes of tomatoes, zucchini, tomatillos, and basil. Located just a few hundred yards away from an indoor kitchen and outdoor grill, the beds are like a private, customized farmers' market. Farther into the property, deer wander along mown pathways in an unfenced field.

From the beginning, the couple's garden plan paid little mind to colors beyond green. As a result, all their planting beds feature a similar foundational structure of low boxwood, herbaceous borders, and tightly knit groundcovers. A grouping of pots encircling a figurative statue contains a predominance of pink annuals one year and orange annuals the next. As a florist, Nutley is known throughout Ulster County for his cornucopian bouquets, and he treats his beds as if they were grand vases filled with choreographed arrangements.

Urso, a jeweler, refers to the style of their tailored, retro living room as "granny moderne," and the same nostalgic aesthetic is evident outside. The couple's shared design confidence enables them to combine anything they

OPPOSITE In David Urso and Dennis Nutley's upstate New York garden, a wicker chair is surrounded by an arbor of hops, arborvitae, pots of scented geranium, basil, lavender, azalea, and pineapple sage.

Twin rabbits guard the front steps of the house, which was built in the 1920s from a Sears Crescent kit.

CLOCKWISE FROM LEFT:

A weathered urn backed by a lattice, an arbor of hops, and a row of arborvitae screens the car court from the garden.

A tree peony (*Paeonia suffruticosa*) retains its texture long after going to seed.

From early summer into fall, vibrant zinnias are peppered throughout the garden.

love, making it easy to imagine their interior collections of framed silhouetted profiles and landscape paintings hanging somewhere outside. Mementos of relatives cover inside surfaces, paralleling the euonymus, lilacs, hostas, pachysandras, and vincas Nutley transplanted from his family's garden. As a child, he and his mother teamed up for annual, post-Easter runs to a local cemetery, where they salvaged discarded pots of azaleas, daffodils, and hyacinths. He looks back on her ingenuity and horticultural savvy with pride: "I remember walking past our garden with my friends after we'd all get off the school bus, and I'd get puffed up. It represented a way to excel." ↓

CLOCKWISE FROM TOP LEFT:

A 1950s-era chandelier hangs above a wrought-iron table and chairs of the same period on the screened-in back porch that faces the gardens on three sides. A hand-built ceramic gooney bird sculpture by Debbie Traeger perches on a rafter.

A weathered birdhouse attracts robins as it balances on the rustic fence next to the main garden gate, between an arborvitae and a large catalpa tree.

A gravel-carpeted dining area with a vintage wrought-iron table and chairs, bordered by Japanese forest grass, pruned boxwood, hydrangea, and several perennials, is the couple's preferred spot for weekend lunches.

FROM LEFT TO RIGHT:

Vivid coleus leaves offset the rungs of a faux-bois concrete bench.

Papyrus and rosemary surround a bronze Art Deco figurine in front of the cement bench, while a cement rooster looks as if it's about to crow.

Pots of lavender, rosemary, coleus, and various succulents are artistically grouped around three old birdhouses Nutley found on-site and placed on a cement column sculpture cast by Don Ruddy.

Contrast

In design, as in most things, opposites attract. They create a positive friction, a mild form of excitement that sparks visual interest. David Urso and Dennis Nutley work with color, texture, and shape in both their professions, so they know this dynamic well, which is why it is a foundational characteristic of their house and garden. Outside, floral upholstered cushions sit on a black wrought-iron chair, feathery grasses grow next to a concrete bench, and a red pillow jolts a sea of greenery—all contributing to a family of energetic contrasts. Nothing is intended to match too much, and some things are kitsch; some are deliberately dissonant or pleasantly nostalgic. Hard and soft, primary colors and neutrals, gritty and smooth textures all contribute in their disparity. ↓

Japanese maple, cannas, hostas, and other perennials, along with a carefully placed birdcage filled with English ivy, contribute to a lush bed bordering a koi pond.

Nutley weeds the dahlia patch before he harvests a basket full of tomatoes, parsley, and Sicilian zucchini.

CLOCKWISE FROM RIGHT:

The moss-covered roof of the potting shed complements the structure's peeling paint and a recently acquired terra-cotta sun plaque.

Nutley transplanted a bed of pachysandra from his family's garden.

On hot summer days, Hans, a long-haired cream dachshund, often cools off in one of several vegetable patches.

FURTHER READING

Barry, Barbara. 2012. *Around Beauty*. New York: Rizzoli.

Benson, Dianne. 1994. *Dirt: The Lowdown on Growing a Garden with Style*. New York: Dell.

Brandolini, Muriel. 2011. *The World of Muriel Brandolini Interiors*. New York: Rizzoli.

Brookes, John. 2002. *Garden Masterclass*. London: Dorling Kindersley Limited.

———. 2008. *The Essentials of Garden Design*. New York: Alfred A. Knopf.

Buchan, Ursula. 2006. *The English Garden*. London: Frances Lincoln.

Burnett, Frances Hodgson. 1911. *The Secret Garden*. New York: Frederick A. Stokes.

de Wolfe, Elsie. 1913. *The House in Good Taste*. New York: The Century Company.

Gauer, James. 2004. *The New American Dream: Living Well in Small Homes*. New York: Monacelli Press.

Giubbilei, Luciano. 2016. *The Art of Making Gardens*. London, New York: Merrell Publishers.

goop.com. N.d. "Inside the Gardens of Luciano Giubbilei." https://goop.com/wellness/food-planet/inside-the-gardens-of-luciano-giubbilei.

Hicks, David. 1979. *Living with Design*. New York: William Morrow and Company.

———. 2003. *My Kind of Garden*. Suffolk, U.K.: Woodbridge.

Hobson, Penelope. 2002. *The Story of Gardening*. London: Dorling Kindersley Limited.

Hoffman, Donald. 1986. *Frank Lloyd Wright: Architecture and Nature*. New York: Dover Publications.

Jekyll, Gertrude. 1984. *On Gardening*. Boston: David. R. Godine.

———. 1899. *Wood and Garden. Notes and Thoughts, Practical and Critical, of a Working Amateur*. Reprint. Charleston, S.C.: CreateSpace Independent Publishing Platform, 2016.

Kaufmann, Edgar, and Ben Raeburn. 1960. *Frank Lloyd Wright: Writings and Buildings*. New York: Meridian Books.

Lloyd, Christopher. 1985. *The Well-Tempered Garden: Wisdom and Advice from a Legendary Gardener*. New York: Random House.

Massey, Anne. 1990. *Interior Design of the 20th Century*. London: Thames & Hudson.

McCarthy, Brian, and Bunny Williams. 2015. *Parish-Hadley Tree of Life: An Intimate History of the Legendary Design Firm*. New York: Stewart, Tabori & Chang.

Myers, Mary. 2009. *Andrea Cochran: Landscapes*. New York: Princeton Architectural Press.

Oudolf, Piet. 2011. *Landscapes in Landscapes*. New York: Thames & Hudson.

Page, Russell. 1962. *The Education of a Gardener*. New York: Atheneum.

Plumptre, George. 1994. *The Garden Makers: The Great Tradition of Garden Design from 1600 to the Present Day*. New York: Random House.

Rosa, Joseph. 1999. *Albert Frey, Architect*. New York: Princeton Architectural Press.

Rudofsky, Bernard. 1964. *Architecture Without Architects: A Short Introduction to Non-Pedigreed Architecture*. New York: Doubleday & Company.

Sackville-West, Vita, and Sarah Raven. 2014. *Sissinghurst: Vita Sackville-West and the Creation of a Garden*. New York: St. Martin's Press.

Saward, Jeff. 2002. *Magical Paths: Labyrinths & Mazes in the 21st Century*. London: Mitchell Beazley Publishers.

Smith, Jane S. 1982. *Elsie de Wolfe: A Life in the High Style (The Elegant Life and Remarkable Career of Elsie de Wolfe, Lady Mendl)*. New York: Atheneum.

Trocmé, Suzanne. 1999. *Influential Interiors: Shaping 20th Century Style Through Key Interior Designers*. New York: Clarkson Potter.

Van Der Host, Arend Jan. 1995. *Art of the Formal Garden*. London: Cassell.

Whitsey, Fred. 2007. *The Garden at Hidcote*. London: Frances Lincoln.

Wohlleben, Peter. 2015. *The Hidden Life of Trees. What They Feel, How They Communicate*. Penguin India.

ACKNOWLEDGMENTS

244   Thanks to all the gardeners, landscape designers, design minds, and property owners whose talent, time, and love of beauty inspired this book—in particular, Marge Brower, Scott Flax, Mark Ripepi, Sari Lampinen, Judy Kameon, Matt Larkin, Hugo Nicole, Bill Georgis, David Urso, Dennis Nutley, Amy Sicis, Carl D'Aquino, Stuart Towner, Scott VanderHamm, Greg Salmeri, Robert Couturier, Brian McCarthy, Danny Sagar, Sarah Draney, Charlie Ferrer, Janice Parker, and the British Society of Garden Designers.

The gorgeous images bring the pages of this book alive, and I salute all the featured photographers, particularly Josh McHugh, Tim Street-Porter, Jamie Midgely, Björn Wallander, Francesco Langnese, Phillip Huynh, Erik Otsea, Clive Nichols, Mick Hales, Alexandra Jane, and Véronique Mati. I'm especially grateful to Laura Hull and John Ellis for their deft camera work as well as their support and encouragement over so many years.

As my very first book was commissioned by Workman Publishing, I'm thrilled to be back in the fold and grateful to all at Timber Press for the care and attention they've paid to creating this book, especially Michael Dempsey, Sarah Milhollin, Lisa Theobald, Hillary Caudle, and the publicity team led by Besse Lynch and Katlynn Nicolls. Heartfelt thanks to Stacee Gravelle Lawrence for, once again, generously and graciously guiding me through the process.

PHOTOGRAPHY CREDITS

Cary Beardow, courtesy of Neil Sutcliffe, page 196 middle

Jennifer Bloch, page 162

Alexandra Davies, pages 104, 105, 106, 108, 109

John Ellis, pages 8, 9, 11, 15, 26, 27, 28, 30, 31, 90, 93, 132, 136, 138, 148, 149, 150, 152, 153, 165

Scott Flax, pages 133, 135, 139

MartinGardner.com, page 48

Mick Hales, pages 174, 175, 176

Laura Hull, pages 50, 94, 95, 96, 98, 99, 101, 103, 188, 189, 190, 191, 192, 193, 194, 195, 200, 201, 202, 204, 205, 206, 207, 209

Phillip Huynh, pages 18, 22 left

Judy Kameon, page 100

Sari Lampinen, Puksipuu, pages 66, 67, 68, 70, 71

Neil Landino Jr., courtesy of Janice Parker Landscape Architects, pages 92 right, 110, 111, 112, 113, 114, 115, 116, 117, 118, 119, 131

Francesco Langnese, pages 54, 60 right, 62

Tony Machado, page 12

Véronique Mati Photographe, pages 182, 183, 184, 185, 187

Joshua McHugh, pages 140, 141, 142, 143, 144, 145, 146

Jamie Midgley, page 10 bottom right

Clive Nichols, pages 224, 225, 226, 228, 229, 230, 231, 232

Hugo Nicole, pages 82, 83, 84, 86, 87, 88, 89

Erik Otsea, page 102

Tim Street Porter, pages 72, 74, 78, 80, 81 top right

Mark Ripepi, pages 32, 34, 36, 37, 38, 40

Paul Rocheleau, courtesy of Matthew Larkin, pages 16, 17, 20, 21, 22 right, 23, 24, 25

Stuart Charles Towner, pages 42, 43, 44, 46, 49

Scott K. VanderHamm, page 158 top left and bottom right

Björn Wallander, pages 2, 166, 168, 171

Raychel Walton, pages 210, 211, 212, 213, 214, 215, 216, 217

⊻

All other photographs are by the author.

INDEX